Eduard Syndicus was born on January 9, 1915, in Hergarten-Eifel, Germany. In 1934 he entered the novitiate of the Society of Jesus. He devoted himself to the study of philosophy and theology until 1948, when he was called for wartime duty, serving as a wireless operator and medical orderly in the Arctic Circle. From 1950-53, he did parish work and studied aesthetics and art history at Munich University, completing his work there in 1954. He is now a lecturer in Christian Art at the Philosophical and Theological College of the Society of Jesus in Frankfurt.

J. R. Foster translated *Early Christian Art* from the German.

EARLY CHRISTIAN ART

IS VOLUME

121

OF THE

Twentieth Century Encyclopedia of Catholicism

UNDER SECTION

XII

CATHOLICISM AND THE ARTS

IT IS ALSO THE

81ST

VOLUME IN ORDER OF PUBLICATION

Edited by HENRI DANIEL-ROPS of the Académie Française

EARLY CHRISTIAN ART

By *EDUARD SYNDICUS*

Translated from the German by J. R. FOSTER

HAWTHORN BOOKS · PUBLISHERS · *New York*

BX
1751
,A1T8
v.121

First Edition, January, 1962.

NIHIL OBSTAT

Carolus Davis, S.T.L.

Censor Deputatus

IMPRIMATUR

E. Morrogh Bernard

Vicarius Generalis

Westmonasterii, die XXV NOVEMBRIS, MCMLXI

The Nihil obstat and the Imprimatur are a declaration that a book or pamphlet
is considered to be free from doctrinal or moral error. It is not implied that
those who have granted the Nihil obstat and Imprimatur agree with the contents,
opinions, or statements expressed.

CONTENTS

CHAPTER I

THE ART OF THE CATACOMBS

We know now from the brilliant history of Christian art, with its cathedrals and ikons, that it is quite capable of giving visible form to the spiritual message of revelation and of facilitating the encounter with the divine, but the leading Christians of the early Church doubted until well into the third century, and with good reason, that such art was possible or permissible. At the end of the second century, in one of Minucius Felix's dialogues, the pagan Caecilius says to the Christian Octavius: "You Christians are primitive. You have no altars, no temples." And Octavius proudly replies: "What temple could I build for God, seeing that the whole world, the work of his own hands, cannot contain him? Should we not rather build a sanctuary for him in our hearts?" When the pagan Celsus writes round about A.D. 180, "You cannot bear to look upon temples, altars or images," seventy years later Origen still replies with the Old Testament prohibition of images, and adds: "Therefore Christians not only have a horror of temples, altars and images; they are even ready to die, if need be, rather than profane their conception of God by doing anything which is forbidden."

Christianity came from the Jews. Christ had not set aside the Law, but fulfilled it. So the first commandment still seemed to be valid: "Thou shalt not carve thyself images, or fashion the likeness of anything in heaven above, or on earth beneath, or in the waters at the roots of the earth" (Deut. 5. 7; Exod. 20. 4). This did not refer to works of art as a whole, for Yahweh revealed himself elsewhere as a God of artists, who filled Bese-leel with his divine spirit, with every kind of craftsmanship and with the artistry to design everything necessary for the taber-nacle (Exod. 31). Solomon's temple possessed giant cherubims of gilded olive-wood, doors adorned with carvings in high relief and bronze basins standing on huge oxen. What was forbidden was the actual image of God, especially in sculpture, and the magic image of a creature; and for very good reasons. Portrayal confers power. When man fashions something he fashions it after his own image, and God's glory and incompre-hensibility are thereby necessarily diminished. Portrayal gives a concrete form to what can only be thought of as infinite life. The image can become an idol which possesses worth and power, and demands respect itself instead of pointing to God. The Jews lived amidst peoples who had long since fallen victims to the danger of magic. They too were tempted to prefer to the abstract God of revelation divinities to which one could cling. For the image holds the god fast and binds him to one spot. Man wins power over him. The prophet had had to wage a hard struggle against the forbidden cult of images, until Yahweh finally weaned his people from them by means of severe punishments. For this reason after the time of the Machabees the Jews rejected more and more decisively any kind of artistic representation at all. It is well known how sensitively they reacted when the Romans brought their legionary standards into Palestine.

Christ had said nothing about art. He had demanded the worship of the Father in the spirit and in truth, and had ascribed less importance to a definite place of worship. He was the living ikon of God, the image of the Father. The Gospel described the spiritual side of his being; it did not provide any information at all about his physical appearance. This unique divine revelation came to an end with his ascension, and the one important thing seemed to be to keep alive his memory, the celebration of the rites, the divine drama, not the divine image.

In their missionary work the apostles became acquainted with the dangerous power of pagan cult-images. Paul nearly lost his life through Diana of Ephesus. In Athens he found the educated classes very enlightened but the people clung, as they had in days gone by, to the physical representation of the divine in innumerable cult-images. In Rome there were close on four hundred temples. New mystery religions were continually arriving from the East, and these cults worked on all the senses through images. Emperor-worship made the encounter with pagan images unavoidable. From the time of Caligula onwards divine honours had to be paid to the statue of the emperor. When an emperor took office statues of him were sent to all the provinces, solemnly inducted and honoured with incense and acclamation. The image represented the emperor, and failure to respect it was regarded as high treason. Many Christians were martyred because they refused to burn a pinch of incense before the emperor's statue.

The Christians of the primitive Church awaited the return of Christ. For them, art was not one of the things that mattered. Their relationship with it consisted mainly in attacking idols. Artists who had become Christians inspired only mistrust. Tertullian advised them to become craftsmen. When the pagan Celsus explained sensibly that the image was not regarded as equivalent to what it represented but was necessary to hint at the invisible, Christians replied, in the spirit of Neo-platonism, that man could only draw nearer to God in so far as he rose above the world of the senses. According to Clement of Alexandria, God had created only one image, his Son. Of this Son there can be only living images, Christians, who grow to resemble him by their virtues. That is the attitude of the early Church. It is as well to keep it in mind, so as not to overlook the limits of representation and the dangers to which it can give rise.

In spite of this, Christian art was bound to come sooner or later. It is difficult for us to imagine the delight which the ancients found in pictures. Today the walls of a room are

papered or painted in one colour or in a quiet pattern; in those days rooms were broken up architecturally by imaginative or decorative painted designs, enlarged by scenes in perspective, and these halls, verandahs and bowers swarmed with painted doves, peacocks, lions, panthers, fishes, cupids, shepherds, sailors, idylls, myths and fairy-tales. The richer Christians had lived in rooms like these before their conversion, and no one demanded that after it they should have all the walls painted over. They recognized how easily most of these themes could be endowed with a Christian meaning. The

On the grave of a mother and daughter

dove became the symbol of the redeemed soul, the peacocks, as before, the symbol of immortality, the fish was the eucharistic food, the shepherd was Christ, and Orpheus, the tamer of

Fish of the living

animals, pointed forward to the Prince of Peace. The beautiful story of Cupid, who wakes Psyche from the sleep of death and leads her to immortality, could be retained. It was the same with the pictorial representations of the seasons. If, in the Praetexta catacomb, young girls pick spring flowers, cherubs bring in the harvest, press the grapes and in winter gather the olives, that is because Christians saw in the change and decay of nature the higher law that we must die in order to gain immortality. All this was confirmed by the teaching of the second-century apologists that Christians need forgo nothing that was noble in humanity. Many of these little pictures of plenty are so stylized and neatly symmetrical in form that they are probably connected with the miniatures mentioned by Clement of Alexandria in the third book of the *Educator*. He says to Christians: "You need a seal-ring just as much as non-Christians do. What motifs can you have engraved on it? Not gods or emblems of war, for we are peace-loving people, not Dionysian figures or pretty girls, but doves, fishes, ships, harps, anchors."

If Clement had to give this encouragement between 203 and 211 on his own initiative, that was because pictorial representations were still rare among Christians. But it is not legitimate to conclude from these small secular works of art that the Christian tradition had still not produced any art at all. It is certainly noteworthy that shepherd and Orante (suppliant) are not mentioned. They were therefore not yet the favourite images of Christians. But about the same time Tertullian, who had fallen into Montanism, criticizes Catholics for making the parable of the lost sheep an excuse for a lax attitude towards penance and for using cups on which the shepherd with the sheep on his shoulder was depicted (*De pudic.* 7).

The ancient delight in pictures was a prerequisite but not the origin of Christian art. There must be organic reasons why, in the midst of persecution, the Christians abandoned their reserved attitude, overcame the strong objections in their scriptures and traditional teaching, and decorated their graves and places of worship with paintings. They must have recognized that art can serve not only beauty but also truth, that it can be creed and proclamation, the expression of faith and hope, and thus prayer. The oldest Christian paintings are in fact prayers of praise, thanks and supplication like the *Gloria* of the Mass: *Tu solus sanctus, tu solus dominus, tu solus altissimus*. In the third century the liturgy was crystallizing. It was creating concrete

forms of expression
for the encounter with
God, and thus also
stimulated art to hint at
the invisible in visible
symbols. Baptism and
the Eucharist were the
sources of Christian
art.

The initiative came
from the laity rather
than from the eccle-
siastical authorities.
The earliest and best
pictures were to be
found not in the cata-

Live in God (gold glass)

combs but in private houses and chapels. Unfortunately almost
no examples of this art, which served the living, have been preserved, except for a few beautiful gold glasses. We have to make
do with the art of the catacombs, which served the dead and
illustrated Christian belief more from the point of view of the
life to come.

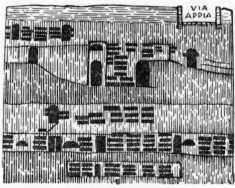

San Callisto catacomb

Two of the most
influential factors
in the creation of
this earliest Christ-
ian art were pagan
tombstones and
the artistic tradi-
tion of the Jewish
Diaspora. Tomb-
stones often bore
portraits, and they
also reflected par-
ticularly clearly the

altered attitude to life of late antiquity. The most important things are no longer life and death, but death and resurrection. The mystery religions showed in their rites and ritual pictures the beatific life after death in Elysium. Burial vaults were transformed by coloured patterns of lines on a white background into boundless, friendly paradises, enlivened by symbols of the seasons, cherubs, flowers and animals, with the most important spaces left free for pictures of the mysteries. This kind of decoration, popular with both pagans and Jews, formed the starting-point, in the late second and early third century, of the earliest Christian art that we know. The dry, white tufa of the walls of ancient Rome has preserved it until today in a more or less reasonable condition in about seventy subterranean "cemeteries", that is, dormitories. No Christian can walk without a feeling of reverence through this city of the dead, the resting-place of so many martyrs. The catacombs consist of long, narrow passages with four to eight graves on top of each other, interspersed with little cubicles for family burials or particularly honoured martyrs, and adorned with homely, inspired emblems of peace, hope, prayer and even joy, signs of optimism in face of the ancient world's fear of destruction, signs of comradeship in the trials of persecution, inscriptions on graves which spring, as Mommsen says, from life itself. (see illustration 3). Some of the earliest catacombs can hardly be distinguished from pagan burial-places. The frescoes of the Lucina vault, the sacramental chapels of San Callisto, so named because of their scenes showing meals, the vault of St Domitilla and

Safe journey with Christ

some others have the same pattern of lines on a white ground, the same pictures of plenty, flowers and gay animals, symbols of the seasons, Orantes and shepherds carrying lambs, a landscape over the arcosolium (niche grave). But at the vertex of the ceiling we find a theme from Revelation, perhaps Daniel amid the lions, soon afterwards the Good Shepherd, and on the walls scenes from the Old and New Testaments (see illustration 2).

In the Old Testament scenes the pregnant form shows that they are the fruit of a fairly long tradition. The Jews of the Diaspora were more broad-minded about pictures. In a Jewish catacomb at Rome the usual geniuses, peacocks and rams

In peace

appear by the side of biblical scenes. Jewish delight in pictures was probably even greater in Hellenistic Alexandria. It may be assumed that in this centre of biblical scholarship there were illustrated manuscripts of almost all the books of the Old Testament. What treasures perished

in this metropolis can be guessed from the surprising chance discovery of Dura-Europos, a remote Roman frontier fortress on the middle Euphrates. This little town was captured and sacked by the Persians in the year 256. To strengthen the town walls the Romans had previously knocked down and filled in several houses, including three places of worship. They were discovered and excavated in 1931. The oldest, the temple of the gods of Palmyra, contains a wall-painting dating from A.D. 75, "The sacrifice of Conon", which reminds one, in its severe and solemn directness, of Ravenna. The Christian place of worship was set up in 232 in the house of one Dositheos. The room for the celebration of the sacrifice remained uncompleted. On the apse-shaped back wall of the baptistery, over the font, there was a picture of the Good Shepherd with twelve sheep.

Underneath were Adam and Eve: the fall and redemption of mankind. There were also pictures of David and Goliath, the Samaritan woman, the healing of the cripple, Christ on the water and the wise virgins. If such a rich cycle of pictures was painted in this lonely frontier town in 232, the beginnings of Christian art cannot lie as late as the art of the Roman catacombs would suggest.

Finally, the synagogue of Dura, built in 244–5, was uncovered, and this was the most important discovery of all. The ceiling was divided into quadrants and decorated with flowers, fruit, birds, gazelles, sea-horses and centaurs. The walls contained, in several bands, one above the other, rich cycles of pictures illustrating Genesis and the stories of Moses, Elias, Ezechiel, Samuel and Esther. There are also some strangers among the patriarchs: the musician Orpheus and winged victories on Aaron's cloak. The

Moses

Old Testament veto on pictures has been completely forgotten. The style shows that the Jews had begun to transform the Hellenistic story-in-pictures into something more symbolic. The scenes are clear, austere compositions springing from the imagination. The huge form of Moses, dressed in a yellow robe, opening up the waters of the Red Sea before the host of the Israelites, leaves an unforgettable impression. So do the figures of the Esther story in their robes of cool red and pink, dark blue and gold, on warm green meadow-land. Similar pictures are to be found in Malta, Sicily and Sardinia, on the coast of Africa and up the Nile. They may well have served as a stimulus to Christian art and hastened its renunciation of subjects taken from everyday life. At Rome, many motifs come and go, so it is unlikely that they originated there. The most important themes are these:

Adam and Eve by the tree of knowledge. This theme appears in an early picture of the San Gennaro catacomb at Naples; it does not occur at Rome until later. An imperial coin with Jason and Medea stealing the golden fleece from a serpent coiled round a tree shows how helpful classical imagery could be.

Noah praying in the ark, which is depicted as a small box. According to Greek mythology, heroes had often been left to perish on the sea in chests of this sort. There is nothing heroic in this picture, no dramatic presentation of the deluge. Only through renunciation of Greek form could Noah with his outstretched arms become a symbol pointing to the world of faith.

Adam and Eve
(*Gold glass*)

The sacrifice of Isaac. In one of the sacramental chapels of San Callisto, Abraham and Isaac stand as Orantes with arms stretched wide apart like priests at the altar of sacrifice. The ram completes the group, making it perfectly symmetrical and reminding us of the Lamb of God. This picture, too, does not simply tell a story; it hints at a mystery. In the catacomb of Priscilla, Isaac with his heavy burden of wood points forward to Christ and his cross.

Moses striking water from the rock. The great figure of Moses stands by the rock. Only the essential is given: the abundance of the water of life.

Daniel saving Susanna. On the left-hand wall of the antechamber of the *Capella greca* (Greek chapel) in the catacomb of St Priscilla there is a painting of the waylaying of Susanna by the two elders. Since then the Renaissance artists have often depicted this incident in sultry tones. In this picture Susanna stands praying between the two men. On the right-hand wall the elders are laying their hands in accusation

Noah. Marble fragment

on her head. A third picture shows her by Daniel's side, saved; both of them are depicted as Orantes. In the Praetexta catacomb, she appears as a lamb between two wolves (see illustration 6).

Daniel in the lions' den. For this neat, symmetrical composition, too, there were many models in classical art.

The three young men in the fiery furnace. They wear eastern clothes, the so-called Phrygian costume: long trousers, a short belted tunic and a tall cap. They stand over the flames with outstretched, crossing arms; for example, in a niche-grave in the Priscilla catacomb.

The story of Jonas is often told in several pictures or in a broad pictorial strip. It is one of the few subjects which leave room for the depictions of nature; perhaps that was why it was so popular. We see the sailors casting Jonas into the sea—often straight into the whale's mouth—the fish spewing him out, and Jonas resting under the arbour. He looks like the handsome shepherd Endymion, who was visited by the moon-goddess.

The same idea underlies all these Old Testament pictures; they are prayers for salvation. It is not God who is depicted, but the powerful protection which he extends to his elect. In prayers for the dying which have come down to us the elect are enumerated as though in a litany:

Lord, save the soul of your servant as you saved Henoch and Elias from universal death ... as you saved Noah from the flood,

Abraham from Ur of the Chaldees, Job from his suffering, Isaac from sacrifice . . ., Lot from Sodom and the flaming fire, Moses from the hand of Pharaoh . . ., Daniel from the lions' den, the three youths from the fiery furnace and the hand of the wicked king, Susanna from the false accusation, David from the hand of king Saul and from the hand of Goliath, Peter and Paul from their prisons.

The facts of the story of salvation are regarded as the only certainty in a transitory world; the hope of paradise as a refuge amid early catastrophes.

The pictures from the New Testament, too, are partly prayers for salvation. In the Apostolic Constitutions the courage to embrace martyrdom and the hope of immortality are strengthened by reference to God, who creates life and can give it afresh to the dead: Adam and Eve formed out of clay, Jonas rescued from the belly of the fish after three days, the bones brought to life in Ezechiel's vision, the miracle of the birth of Christ from a virgin, the young man of Naim and Jairus's daughter, the healing of the man sick of the palsy, the raising of Lazarus, the miracle at Cana and the multiplication of the loaves. The miracle of the birth of Christ from the Virgin Mary is evoked by the early picture of the Annunciation in the catacomb of St Priscilla. A youth, still without wings, reverently approaches the sitting Virgin. Another picture in the same catacomb speaks more clearly. Above the oldest picture of the Madonna that we know, a very vigorous mother feeding her lusty child, stands the star of Jacob, the sign of the saviour. Bileam points to it. The Magi bear witness to the fulfilment of the prophecy.

Figures who appear often are the man sick of the palsy, healed and carrying home his bed, and the risen Lazarus, still wrapped in the grave-clothes or else already undone and standing in front of his sepulchre.

But salvation from the stress of earthly life and hope of peace in heaven are not the only themes. Some of the pictures already mentioned and many others speak of the new life conferred by baptism and strengthened by the Eucharist which the redeemed enjoy already.

The early pictures of the baptism of Christ reminded Christians of their own baptism. In one of the so-called sacramental chapels of San Callisto a ship in a storm can be seen above the picture of the baptism of Christ. One figure is being hauled on board, another saved from above. Tertullian tells us that many commentators on Scripture wanted to see a symbol of baptism in the storm on the sea described in the Gospels, but he rejects this idea. For Cyprian, too, baptism is salvation from the "waves of the storm-tossed world" (*Ad Donat.* 3). The fisherman on the bank of the Jordan—a favourite picture—is Christ, "fisher of men, who tempts the holy fish out of the hostile waters with the sweet bait of life" (Clement of Alexandria, *Paed.* 3, 101, 3). A particularly beautiful example of these fishing pictures occurs in the oldest Christian mosaic in a mausoleum under St Peter's; it is made of blue stones set in a gold background, and dates from about A.D. 280. Baptism was called φωτισμός, illumination. For this reason the figure of the teacher appears beside the picture of baptism. He speaks to the Samaritan woman about the water of life. The water of salvation is prefigured in the water from the rock or in the pool of Siloe, whose waters received healing powers from the angel. The man sick of the palsy who was healed in the pool usually appears near the pictures of baptism.

The many pictures of meals were at first interpreted only too readily as referring to the Eucharist. And it is precisely here, so it seems, that often enough popular piety and popular usage provided the stimulus. Many of these scenes are funeral feasts— the pagans held them, too—with plentiful food and drink in honour of the dead. We learn from St Augustine that this "comforting of the dead" could not be suppressed even by severe prohibitions. At Rome the number of participants was usually seven, so the meal with seven men and two big wine-jars (under San Sebastiano) should not necessarily be interpreted as the meal by the Lake of Tiberias.

These funeral feasts, known as *refrigeria*, were at the same time images of the heavenly meal desired for the dead in the place of refreshment, the *locus refrigerii*, in accordance with Christ's promise: "I allot to you a place to eat and drink at my table in my kingdom" (Luke 22. 29). One series of these pictures does expressly depict the meal of the blessed. Vibia is led by an angel into paradise and shares in the eternal marriage-feast.

Adoration of the Magi (Gravestone of Severa)

Agape and Irene, love and peace, serve the guests. On the table usually lies the fish, the eucharistic food (see illustration 4).

A third series of meal pictures still remains extremely impressive: the man in San Callisto stretching his hands out over the bread and wine, while a woman stands praying at his side; the feeding of the five thousand by Christ and the apostles (in San Sebastiano), who carry away seven baskets of crumbs; or simply the fish before the basket of bread and the beaker of red wine—the messianic banquet of the Jews: all these subjects signify the community with Christ and in the last resort the Eucharist as the vital nourishment of the soul. Seeing that the Eucharist was kept secret even from catechumens, the great variety of veiled allusions to it proves what a central position this most precious legacy of the Lord occupied in Christian life. "O fish, be merciful to me; I long for thee, my Lord and Redeemer!" (inscription on the grave of Pectorio).

Other groups of pictures fit easily into this framework. The early pictures of the Annunciation, the adoration of the Magi, at which Balaam is usually present as their spiritual forebear and prophet from the ranks of the pagans, all express joy at the coming of God and his sojourn among men, at the merciful summons of pagans, too, to share in the light of life.

The experience of earthly difficulties and divine help, of being "in distress yet not abandoned" gained concrete expression at an early period in the primitive Church.

THE SHEPHERD

The figure of the Good Shepherd was easily the most popular symbol of salvation among Christians of this century. More than three hundred pictures and statues of shepherds have been preserved. Both Old and New Testament provided good grounds for the use of this theme. God had fulfilled his promise given in Ezechiel: "I myself will come and feed my sheep." Like David, his ancestor, Christ had protected his people from the beasts of prey. The shepherd brings salvation. Because salvation begins with baptism, his picture adorns the baptistery of Dura-Europos on the Euphrates. It was present in the baptistery of St Peter's built by Damasus. It is present in the erstwhile portico of the Lateran baptistery, and four times in San Giovanni in fonte at Naples. Baptism was known as σφραγίς, sealing or branding. Just as the shepherd brands his animals with the monogram of their owner, so the divine Shepherd has stamped Christians with the ineradicable seal. A Syrian baptismal formula runs like this: "X is herewith baptized, that he may be a lamb of the flock of Christ, in the name of the Father. . . ." The Roman liturgy expresses the same idea by putting Good Shepherd Sunday immediately after Low Sunday,[1] the feast of the newly baptized. The Good Shepherd guides us with reliable teaching, says Aberkios, the "disciple of the divine Shepherd". That is why the otherwise very youthful shepherd sometimes has a beard, wears the pallium and carries the teacher's papyrus-roll. In a fresco under San Sebastiano, he returns to the flock and to the neighbours, as saviour of sinners, with the sheep that has gone astray. He carries the dead safely along the dangerous road referred to in the old offertory of the Mass for the dead, "through the darkness, over the abyss, past the jaws of the lion", to the fields of light.

Christian as all this seems today, the picture of the Good Shepherd could never have fulfilled its important task if antiquity had not contributed its imagery and ideas, and indeed even stimulated a deeper interpretation. Ancient art had produced an abundance of shepherd-pictures, from the rustic,

The Shepherd (Gravestone of Gerontius)

romantic idyll to amazingly profound statements about the divine and universal reason which, embodied as the logos-shepherd, saves and feeds souls and leads them back to the divine ground. The coin commemorating the millenary of Rome in 248 showed such a saviour-shepherd with seven sheep. Just as St John makes use of the logos idea in his prologue as a correct pagan presentiment of Christ, the incarnate wisdom and love of God, so Clement of Alexandria and

[1] *Dominica in deponendis albis*, the Sunday on which the white baptismal robes are laid aside.

other Fathers of the Church take over the logos-shepherd idea: "We can come to know the perfect wisdom of the holy shepherd and educator, the omnipotent logos of the Father, where he uses an image and calls himself a shepherd of the flock" (*Paed.* I. 84, 1–85, 2).

The Logos is the divine nature of Christ. That is why the famous statuettes in the Lateran museum and most other portraits of the shepherd portray him as the ancients imagined their gods, young and handsome, symbols of immortality. The lamb on his shoulder stands for raised and redeemed human nature. "The Logos, the eternal word of the Father, came down from heaven to seek the sheep that was lost, man, whom he had formed in his own image and likeness. And the shepherd found his lamb in the womb of the virgin and carried it obediently right up to the sacrifice on the cross, in order to lead it joyfully back to the flock of life, the good shepherd who has found the lost sheep, the high priest who has brought the lamb to sacrifice" (Irenaeus, *Adversus Haereses*, V, 16, 3).

Many such examples can be adduced from early Christian writing, but the previously mentioned biblical ideas occupied the foreground. The shepherd must have been the picture most frequently found in places of worship before Constantine.

ORANTE

A female figure with raised hands, in the ancient attitude of prayer, is often found facing the shep-
herd. It, too, is well known to us from pagan art from the fourth century before Christ onwards. In the reign of Augustus this figure appears on coins as *Pietas Augusti*. The early Church made it into the personification of the prayer for salvation, as the occasional inscription εὐχή, prayer, shows. If the shepherd is

Mary as Orante

the divine saviour, the female figure praying represents humanity raising its arms in its need to the saviour. In other cases the Orante represents a dead person, for whom a swift entry into paradise is desired—only the martyrs were believed to attain immediate bliss—or who is asked for his prayers to God. "Atticus, you are already in paradise, pray for your parents!" A beautiful expression of the communion of saints.

The third and deepest meaning of the Orante is already recognizable on the ceiling of the Lucina vault, one of the

Orans

oldest paintings of all. In the panels of the design the logos-shepherd and the Orante in a bridal veil appear twice each: as Irenaeus says, shepherd of the saved and bridegroom of the Church. The Church as the bride of Christ is an idea that was very much alive in the third century. On fourth-century sarcophagi she stands in a thoughtful attitude beside the living Christ, or praying between Peter and Paul. In the mosaic of Santa Sabina (about 425) she becomes the teaching Church. One panel in the wooden door there combines all this in one grand design. Above, in the circle of heaven. is Christ as the mighty Lord of the second coming, between the apocalyptic symbols. Underneath is the earthly sky. Here the Orante stands under the cross, which Peter and Paul hold up, as the expectant Church. She knows that her path, too, will lead through the cross to glory (see illustration 22).

The Orante sums up the basic theme of all early Christian art: man praying before God who brings salvation.

ORPHEUS

On the gravestone of Gerontius in the catacomb of Domitilla, Christ as shepherd sits playing the pan-pipes, at his feet a sheep listening to him. The oldest frescoes in the catacombs of St Callistus and St Priscilla have similar pictures of Orpheus, the mythical singer, surrounded by sheep. Imagery developed by the Orphic sect under Jewish influence is here taken over. Later on we find Orpheus taming wild animals with

Orpheus

his singing. Clement of Alexandria is familiar with this picture and gives it a charming application to Christ: it was only the heavenly Word, the true fighter in the good fight, who wins the victor's laurels in the theatre of the whole world, who could tame man, the wildest of animals: not only birds—the light-minded—and creeping creatures—the deceitful—but also lions —the bad-tempered—swine—the sensual—and wolves—the rapacious. See what the new song has done: out of stones and animals it has made man. And those who were dead came to life as soon as ever they heard the singing (*Protr.* 1. 4. 4).

This interpretation was occasionally applied to the Good Shepherd. In the Praetexta catacomb we can see on one side his flock and on the other the donkey and the pig, who symbolize the passions. On a sarcophagus in Gerona the long series of pictures of Christ standing on a lion or dragon begins. Eusebius quotes: "Thou wilt tread on serpents and adders and crush the lion and the dragon. . . . What were these animals but the heads of demons?"

THE TEACHER

The last decades of the third century and the early decades of the fourth favour pictures of Christ as teacher and educator as well as shepherd. The spiritual stimulus was provided by the debate with pagan philosophy, in which Christians felt confident of victory, and the imagery by the writings of the pagan philosophers themselves. To the century of Plotinus, the struggle for wisdom seemed the surest way to immortality.

Christ has brought the true knowledge of God which leads to salvation. There is a picture of him as shepherd and teacher in the Hypogaeum on the Viale Manzoni. He sits between sheep and goats and reads a roll of manuscript. Aberkios calls himself a disciple of the divine Shepherd who leads his flocks to pasture on the mountains and plains and has great eyes that see through everything. This shepherd has imparted to him knowledge that can be relied upon. The picture of the teacher now sometimes occupies the important place at the vertex of the vault. He wears the pallium and carries a papyrus roll. All round are pictures of miracles, the strong arguments of his true philosophy. In San Callisto he sits with the papyrus roll opposite the Samaritan woman. In the Cemeterium Maius he and six apostles recall the seven wise men of antiquity. He has made the wisdom of antiquity superfluous: "Through him, the logos, the whole world has become Athens and Greece", says Irenaeus (*Adversus Haereses*, IV, 22, 31). Sometimes it is eight apostles, but more often the Twelve. This picture was very often painted in the niches of catacombs (see illustration 19). It was also frequently used in the apse of early basilicas. Then the image of the teacher merges with that of the law-giver and ruler. It broadens into the apocalyptic and deepens into a genuine mystery picture, becoming a conspectus of salvation on earth and heavenly glory.

Christian sculpture begins in the third century, rather later than painting. The richer Christians retained the custom of putting their dead in marble sarcophagi. In Rome more than five hundred pagan and Christian sarcophagi have been preserved; three hundred have been found in Gaul; and some at Ravenna and other places in the empire. Many are made in the form of a box, others with an architectural shape, as a house for the dead person. Nowhere is the organic link between antiquity and Christianity evident in more concrete form than in these sarcophagi. For sometimes it is impossible to decide whether a sarcophagus is still pagan or already Christian. Before the middle of the century the shepherd who brings salvation appears on the lion sarcophagus between the lions, which are symbols of death. Beside him stand two sheep and he carries a third on his shoulder. The gravestone of Livia Primitiva shows the shepherd returning home, fish and anchor on each side. All this may be, but is not necessarily, Christian. The same is true of the philosopher-sarcophagi which begin to appear about 250. The shocks suffered by the Roman empire in the second half of the third century awoke strong interest in philosophical and religious questions. The intellectual and moral stature of Plotinus, among whose disciples was the Emperor Gallienus, may well have contributed to this situation. One of the earliest and most beautiful of sarcophagi, that of La Gayolle in Gaul, shows a philosopher reading between the Good Shepherd and the praying woman. It is difficult to know whether it is a noble pagan who hoped to gain immortality through piety and striving for wisdom, or a Christian to whom the Gospel showed the path of prayer to Christ the saviour. Do the fisherman and shepherd on each side of the central group signify the beginning and full enjoyment of the new life in Christ, as they do in the catacomb paintings, or do they still express the pagan conception of heaven? The sun-god beside the fisherman would not have worried a Christian. He had long been familiar with anchor and dove.

The no less beautiful sarcophagus of the Via Salaria is flanked by two huge rams. Beside the left-hand one sits the reading philosopher with the features of the dead husband, beside the right-hand one the dead wife with a papyrus roll. Orante and shepherd occupy the middle (see illustration 7). Other sarcophagi show the philosopher between symbols of death such as the door of the grave, a sundial, lions or the lovers Cupid and Psyche in paradise. Frequently the Orante occupies the central position in the pastoral paradise.

The sarcophagus of Santa Maria Antiqua is indubitably Christian. Once again we have the philosopher between the shepherd and the Orante, but beside the shepherd is the baptism of Christ as a symbol of the transmission of life, and beside the Orante two scenes showing Jonas, as a visible embodiment of the prayer for salvation. Jonas rests under the arbour in the attitude of the sleeping Endymion.

This sarcophagus was not made to order, but to keep in stock. The unfinished heads of the philosopher and the praying woman were to receive the features of the deceased.

The true philosophy, which must come to terms with the problem of death, leads through prayer to the divine saviour. So the saviour himself soon assumes the form and garb of the philosopher: beard, cloak, papyrus roll and staff (see illustration 10).

The polychrome fragments of the Thermae museum (c. 300) show him several times in a row as preacher and saviour of the poor, as a man of the people and at the same time as one of awe-inspiring dignity. The spiritual portrait of Christ provided by the synoptic Gospels is here for the first time translated into stone. It enables us to understand why the cultured Clement of Alexandria imagined Christ as outwardly inconspicuous, but reflecting a spiritual beauty (see illustration 8). Christian sculpture grows, like Christian painting, out of the belief in immortality. Shepherd and Orante, the oldest symbols of the art of the catacombs, walk by the side of the seeker after truth. Human prayers and divine mercy are to win for him the eternal rest symbolized by the slumbering Jonas.

Sarcophagi portraying Jonas grow very popular towards the end of the period of persecution. Sarcophagus No. 119 in the Lateran museum bears an extremely lifelike and dramatic series of pictures showing the prophet running away from God, being thrown by the sailors to the sea-monster, being cast up and resting under the arbour.

The early catacomb theme, Noah in the chest, is added in miniature. A fishing idyll on the right harks back to pagan tradition, but the resurrection of Lazarus and the legendary spring-miracle of Peter at the top point already to the theme of the first half of the fourth century, Christ the divine miracle-worker.

THE CHARACTER OF THE EARLIEST CHRISTIAN ART

This was bound to be ambiguous. It is true that even later on there was never one individual style for Christian art; contemporary forms were simply taken over, ennobled, spiritualized and elevated in order to express sacred themes; but the Christian tradition, through the wealth of its imagery, does show a good deal of uniformity and stimulate fresh creation. The primitive Church, on the other hand, being an underground Church without the time or the leisure for artistic creation, had to do what it could with the forms of pagan antiquity. This was both a help and a hindrance, in so far as these forms were still those of a dying and degenerate classical art with an indestructible delight in sensuous beauty, an art reflecting enjoyment of life or flight into the idyllic, an art expressing devotion to life. With artistic means of this sort it was difficult to express the supernatural, the holy, the expectation of a world to come. For this reason the oldest Christian art did not aim at being "art". It preferred to be naïve and ugly rather than risk being suspected of wishing to dally with beauty for its own sake. So it begins by neglecting classical form, which in itself had once been so rich in spiritual content. For the sake of new values it reduces the usual wealth of movement and expression. It leaves out charming landscapes and architectural backgrounds. It does not put the scenes it portrays in an earthly, finite perspective. The figures stand flat and incorporeal on the bright background of the wall, which thereby takes on an unearthly quality. They face the spectator directly, removed from the flux of time. They are people possessed by God and reflect his action; guides to God who form, together with the spectator, the holy community of those who believe and know. The content of the picture is taken for granted; it is conveyed in brief, almost schematic signs; abbreviated to initial letters, as it were, not spelled out fully with the perfect clarity of beautiful form.

The pictures are signposts, informative rather than beautiful, often uncouth and primitive, the work of craftsmen rather than artists. It is only occasionally that a portrait of the Virgin Mary or an Orante attains the artistic quality, the inspired expression of the face of a mummy from the Fayyum. The first Christian art is poor in resources. A pot of red ochre and a bit of green are sufficient for its purpose. Preliminary sketches are superfluous. All this cannot be explained, as Riegl would explain it, as the result of a new artistic aim. The gap between intention and achievement is often only too obvious. Yet this renunciation of aesthetic effect, this devotion to meaning, indicates the way in which the Christian art of the West was to develop: from the self-sufficing work of art to the symbol with a spiritual significance.

Memorial art, the only kind that has been preserved, does not provide a balanced picture. The works by better artists in Christian houses and private chapels certainly betrayed more delight in beauty and were much closer to contemporary art.

The anti-classical art of the age of persecution was bound to suffer a setback in the peaceful days of the fourth century. When Christ's kingdom and the Roman empire joined forces, the art forms of the empire, even the official art of the court,

were utilized to such an extent that resemblances to the ancient
cult of images could be traced and the Fathers of the Church
began a fresh onslaught on pictures and statues. Classical or
Hellenistic conceptions of human greatness and imperial dignity
were applied to Christ and his disciples. The biblical stories
were told in the normal style of triumphal art. Even in the
fourth century truly religious works of art were produced on
this post-classical foundation. But it was only in the fifth
century, when the earthly empire was approaching its end and
the Church was forced to remember that it was not of this
world, that it overcame the too earthly character of the classical
style and once again became unclassical, but in a more elevated
way than in the third century. Many elements which had already
appeared here and there in the catacombs, giving then the
impression of incapacity rather than of a deliberate artistic
purpose, now joined forces to express a strong spiritual life
anchored in eternity.

But the transformation of the ancient form by the new content could only be effected so relatively quickly because pagan
art offered assistance in so far as it was *late* classical art. In the
second and third centuries plastic vigour, the feeling for the
organically beautiful, began to weaken. The idea grew more
important than the form. Art became the product of the mind
instead of that of the eye. Its significance no longer emerged
naturally from within; it was something merely added to the
figure. With this diminution of form, action lost its natural
coherence. It had to be thought out rather than seen. The face
and hands were meant to be expressive rather than the body.

The East had always inclined towards this more linear, two-
dimensional, stylized, strictly symmetrical, frontal kind of
portrayal when it wanted to express something hieratic and
solemn, timeless and spiritualized. This kind of art found its
way into the Roman empire by many paths. Popular art in the
provinces had long preferred the more expressive if coarser
style to Greek refinement. From the third century onwards the

universality of the Romano-Hellenistic style was gradually contaminated and altered by the individual characteristics of the different peoples in the empire. It grew more barbaric, but it was also strengthened by fresh invention and stronger gesture.

The decline of classical form corresponded to a changed conception of life. The ancients had accepted good and bad, life and death, from fate in a spirit of pious submission or brave resignation. The Stoics had taught that after a well-filled life one should not be afraid of death. In the third century this confidence in life was badly shaken. Through the soldier-emperors the empire fell a prey to inward confusion and threats from outside. Changes of every kind, oppressive taxes to support the army and the government, a fall in the birth-rate and outbreaks of disease made Italy into a poor country. Eastern religions, such as Mithraism, that believed in a life to come, found numerous adherents.

But it was not so much the catastrophes of the third century as the new valuation of the soul that assisted Christianity and Christian art. Plotinus and others were teaching the most decided anti-materialism. Matter was no longer regarded as the mirror of the spirit, but as a hindrance to it; and therefore it was no longer considered right to express things of spiritual significance in an ideal physical form. The doctrine of the liberation of the soul at death from the fetters of matter and of the return to the divine home was reflected in art in many ways. A new inwardness, a franker reflection of the soul, especially in the eyes, succeeded the cult of physical beauty. Faces speak as never before of the transitory nature of the world, but also of the longing for immortality. This art was able to serve Christianity just as the philosophy of Plotinus served Neo-Platonism. That it was in the middle of this process of transformation explains the lack of unity in early Christian art. But as time went on this variety emerged as an advantage. Greek art, worldly as it was, would not have formed, by itself, a good foundation. As an ingredient, on the other hand, a never-forgotten criterion, it remained of inestimable value to Byzantium and, via Byzantium, to the West. But it could only attain its full effect after other peoples in Syria, Palestine, Egypt, North Africa and, later, northern Europe, had contributed their talent for abstraction and expression. Just as Christianity was the yeast that transformed the social, political and religious pattern of the Roman empire, so it also provided the conditions for one of the greatest revolutions that art has ever undergone. Christianity is just as far removed from rejection of the world as it is from undue devotion to it. It takes this earth seriously as a place of trial, but at the same time it seeks a home in another world of which everything earthly is only a likeness. It knows better than anyone of the threat to man from sin and of his elevation by grace. It demands renunciation now in order to gain everything later. It looks forward, beyond suffering and death, to the transfiguration of the body and the glory of heaven. The Christian must steadfastly overcome appearances. He must regard an invisible spiritual world comprehended by faith as more beautiful and better than the visible, apparently so real and lasting world. In exactly the same way Christian art has to take the path from realism to the symbolism which removes the supernatural from what is only too near and comprehensible. Instead of the harmoniously developed man of antiquity it has to portray the saint touched by the hand of God and gazing into the world of God; instead of the tragic hero, who tries to overcome all resistance with his own strength and is destroyed in the process, the man who prays and struggles humbly and for whom earthly destruction signifies victory. It is no longer man who is the measure of all things but God and his way of salvation.

The content of the Christian message slowly and steadily created a new artistic vocabulary for itself out of the readily adaptable forms of late classical art.

There is no simple answer to the question, where did Christian art originate and to what lands is it most indebted?

We can follow neither Strzygowski and Wulff, who ascribe all creative ideas to the East, nor Wilpert and others, who give all the credit to the West. The appearance and disappearance of so many motifs in Rome suggest the conclusion that they were all imported. But this fluctuation is typical of all capital cities, which assimilate much and reject much, but also attract the guiding influences. In many respects Alexandria provided more favourable conditions—stimuli from both East and West, greater freedom before 313—but no precedence can be proved, for no memorials have been preserved at Alexandria (or at Antioch). Rome early collected all influences, put them in the melting-pot and handed them on to Byzantium in the fourth century. In the fifth century, and even more in the sixth, the East takes a clear lead, for the German invasions robbed Italy for a long period of the tranquillity necessary for artistic creation.

CHAPTER II

THE BASILICA

THE HOUSE OF THE COMMUNITY

Like Paul in Troas (Acts 20. 7), the apostles used to celebrate
the Last Supper and to preach in a big room of a private house.
A table served as altar and a cup as chalice; cross and candles
were not yet in use. Here, too, the saying applied: we have no
abiding home, but seek
the world to come. Lac-
tantius says that true
religion offers no scope
for violence or sacrilege
because its holy of holies
is situated in the spirit.

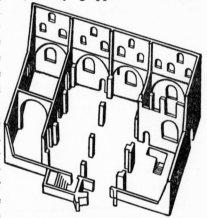

However, as the periods
of tranquillity between
persecutions became long-
er and Christian commun-
ities grew in size, bigger
spaces were needed for the
services, and side-rooms
for the instruction of the

San Martino ai Monti

catechumens and for works of charity. The richer Christians
provided houses which could be converted internally for these
purposes while outwardly remaining private houses. The name
of the founder was also retained as title on the entrance and
later passed over to the church built on the same spot. Round

about the year 200, inconspicuous community-houses of this sort seem to have been built specifically for the purpose. Tertullian already speaks at this time of the "house of God", while Clement of Alexandria still emphasizes that the best temple, God's true sanctuary, is the community of the chosen, not the visible building.

Cyprian employs the word *Kyriakon*—house of the Lord— from which our word "church" is derived. About 230, in the reign of Alexander Severus, the Christians won a lawsuit concerning a piece of ground for a church. In the reign of Decius, "sanctuaries of the Christians" were seized. From this period dates the Titulus Aequitii beside the basilica of San Martino ai Monti, with its big hall divided lengthways by two rows of pillars and its cross-vaulted roof.

Usually house-churches were big rectangular rooms without an apse, divided by a barrier into the spaces for the congregation and the priest. There were certainly also early forms of the later basilica, rectangular halls supported by pillars, with a bulge at one end. They must have approximated to the popular conception of a place of worship, for in Diocletian's persecution we often hear of the destruction of churches. There were certainly proper churches in the lands which enjoyed a fair amount of freedom some time before Constantine: Syria, Edessa in Mesopotamia, Armenia and Persia.

Many spots in Rome still convey a vivid impression of the way the Church grew up out of subterranean darkness into the light.

Beneath the church of St John and St Paul you can walk through houses of the first to third centuries which were joined up into an *insula*, a small block of flats. On the walls you can see naked youths wearing garlands, in the courtyard the beautiful fresco of the marriage of Thetis; you can see the wine-cellar, the bath and the conveniently arranged shops on the south side. At the beginning of the fourth century the owner became a Christian. Christian paintings took their place by the side of the pagan ones; the Orante joined the youths. Later in the fourth century the senator Byzantius installed a chapel on the upper floor. The stairs leading to it were rebuilt. A landing was added in the middle, with a painted niche in honour of the two martyrs who were traditionally supposed to have met their death under these stairs. Over this spot, up above in the chapel, stood the altar, against one of the long sides. It was a hall, not a basilica. Early in the fifth century Pammachius, Byzantius' son, put up heavy supporting walls on the ground floor, filled up the spaces between with rubble, and in place of the upper storey built a three-aisled basilica which made use of the old much-altered south wall. The altar-stone over the martyrs' bones was retained on the right-hand side of the middle aisle. The ground-plan gives a good impression of this much

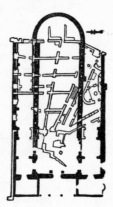

SS. John and Paul

built-on site. The tall tower was erected in the early Middle Ages over the huge portico of the temple of Claudius, which was next door on the northern side.

A trip beneath San Clemente is just as impressive. Deep in the earth, where an underground stream rushes along, one enters a temple of Mithras, with a picture of the god slaying the bull. A vestibule leads to a long line of resting-places that date

San Clemente

from the second century. From there one climbs up into the so-called lower church. Here, about 250, was one of the oldest private chapels, the Titulus Clementis. In the fourth century the regularly shaped house with the pillared halls round it was converted into a big basilica. In the Norman invasion of 1084 this quarter of Rome was destroyed and the débris piled up round San Clemente. Pope Pascal II had the supporting walls put up and the débris shovelled in between them. He then built the present upper church, smaller in size, on the top of the earlier central nave and left-hand aisle. The boundaries of the altar enclosure and the ambos were taken over from the old church (see illustration 13).

In a similar way towards the end of the fourth century St Prisca on the Aventine was built over the Mithraeum of a Roman palace. The connection between Roman civilization and Christianity can be seen clearly in St Balbina, near the

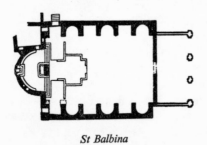

St Balbina

baths of Caracalla. From the inner courtyard of a well-preserved ancient building one enters a wide, lofty hall with an apse. All round it, high up, is a line of big mullioned windows; below, rounded and right-angled niches alternate on the long sides. The secular building was so big and vigorous in conception that only slight alterations were required to convert it into a truly sacramental space.

THE HOUSE OF GOD

After the edict of Milan (313) the Church came out into the open. It had to set up house in this world. The Roman empire became its living-space. Soon the fruitful concept of a Christian

empire arose. The emperor handed over his authority to Christ.
This required visible embodiment in church architecture.
Roman buildings which reflected in impressive form the power
and dignity of the emperor's position were ready to hand:
palaces and baths with splendid suites of rooms, roofed with
bold cross- and barrel-vaulting; circular temples like the
Pantheon, whose mighty domes could represent heaven;
rectangular temples which had been developed from Greek
models into really large covered spaces. But for Christian uses
all these forms were excluded because they had been designed
too unequivocally for their purposes: the worship of idols and
worldly splendour. In those early days the danger of profaning
Christianity was greater than the prospect of sanctifying the
profane. It was not until the difficult days of the sixth and
seventh centuries that some temples at Rome were converted
into churches. Under Justinian the tradition of Roman imperial
architecture was continued in church building. But at Rome the
Pantheon and the basilica of Constantine had to wait for the
architects of the Renaissance to make them the models for the
new St Peter's. To the early Church, only one sort of building
seemed suitable for christianization: the basilica. Public
basilicas were used not for worship but for community life.
Markets, trials and festivals were held in them. They existed in
every form from the soberly functional to the splendidly
decorative. They were rectangular halls, with the roof carried on
pillars and raised in the middle to admit light. Some were of
one storey, others of two; in some the apse, which formed the
focal point, was at the end, in others in the middle of one of the
long sides. In the apse stood the raised platform for the judge
or the leader of the assembly. Many basilicas had two apses.
Many individual details, especially the multiplication of naves
or aisles, occur again in the Christian basilica, but the scholars'
long dispute about the origin of the form as a whole shows that
here no direct path leads from the old to the new. In spite of
the apses and the rectangular form, the public basilica looks

inwards towards the middle. It was not recognized until comparatively recently that the private basilicas of well-to-do families and the palace-basilicas for the emperor or his viceroys

are far more direct precursors of the Christian house of God. It is true that many of them have only one nave, but they all have the entrance at one end and lead the visitor up the length of the hall to the apse with the throne of the emperor or the seat of honour of the master of the house. Three-aisled basilicas of this sort, such as those of Gortyn or Kremna, can hardly be distinguished in ground-plan from Christian ones. The differences lie rather in elevation and general arrangement.

Gortyn

Kremna

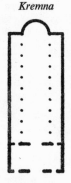

The Christians took over the ground-plan, mode of construction and separate parts of the building, which appealed to them because of its simplicity and clarity, and developed out of them by a genuinely creative process their house of God, a fitting background for the Roman liturgy. Even the first imperial foundation, the church of the Redeemer, begun in 313 and later known as St John Lateran, is a truly original building.

THE LATERAN BASILICA

The secular basilica stood in the midst of the bustle of city life and there were many entrances to it in its long side. The palace basilica formed part of a complex of buildings. The Christian basilica was isolated and divided off from the bustle of the town. The atrium formed a holy precinct between the basilica and the street. The atrium is a private courtyard enclosed by a covered walk open on the inner side, with a well in the middle. Often it is a pretty little garden with pines and cypresses, known as a "paradise", a place of meditation and purification. Next to the atrium is the narthex or portico of the basilica. This is a last barrier. Here catechumens and penitents remain, and from here the doors open into the basilica itself. The plain exterior has already aroused the visitor's expectations. The Greek temple was built to be seen from outside; it was a beautiful casket for the statue of the god. The sacrifice took place outside in the open air. The Christian basilica, on the other hand, looks inwards. It is a community hall arranged for a definite purpose, and the visitor feels this as soon as he enters. With his first glance he measures the width, openness, height and light of the nave, which is protected by the lower side-aisles against the profane world as though by a zone of darkness. Secular art may here and there have made the walls over the middle rows of pillars higher—though this was unthinkable to Vitruvius, and actual examples of it can only be found in round buildings—but it is precisely by means of these high walls that Christian art creates its impression of spiritualization, of weightiness illuminated from above and striving upwards. The space is enclosed on top by a flat ceiling or the bare framework of the roof, with beautifully decorated beams. Gone is the classical balance between support and load upon which Vitruvius had insisted unconditionally even in the basilica. And we already feel how strongly and clearly the space also points forward to the front. Thither lead the processional aisles of the nave, the line of uniformly spaced pillars, the rows of saints in mosaic and fresco above them, and higher still the path of light traced by the windows whose stone tracery is filled with slabs of alabaster or glass. This forward movement flows on through the gateway of the great triumphal arch in the wide transept and comes to rest in the apse. It is not known for certain if the transept of the Lateran church was part of the original building, but certainly its significance was clearly recognized later on. It is the throne-room of Christ the Emperor. Here stands the throne, roofed over by the ciborium like the imperial throne. The semicircle of the apse contains the bishop's cathedra, between the chairs of the priests. The bishop represents Christ when he faces the congregation at the sacrifice. The congregation is gathered like a big family round the altar area, which projects into the nave, enclosed by low barriers and raised pulpits for the reading of the Scriptures. The meaning of the celebration of the mysteries is made visible in the picture in the apse. This first big church mosaic was altered in the sixth century, when the church was dedicated to St John the Baptist, by the addition of the saints. In the ninth century it was seriously damaged, in the thirteenth it was restored by Torriti, and in the nineteenth removed and then replaced. It is the first picture of the Trinity and the first big panorama of the redemption. Right at the top of the clouds there was originally not a cherub but the hand of the Father. Below are the head and shoulders of Christ the mediator, who proceeds from the Father and, through the spirit of love, which proceeds from both, completes on the cross the work of redemption. The jewelled cross on the mountain of paradise points back up at the same time to Christ in his glory. Incarnation, death and resurrection—descent and ascension—are here proclaimed to the congregation in powerful symbolic terms.

The picture points directly to the content of the liturgy, the actualization of the passion and apotheosis of Christ, and illustrates it. It is the first mystery picture, and was to be followed by many others.

In the Lateran basilica, with its five aisles, Constantine's architects realized with amazing insight, and firmly established for the future, the idea of a church leading up to the throne of the Almighty. They separated the altar area from the space for the congregation, articulated the latter more clearly by heightening the central nave, and endowed all the individual parts with unity. Thus a stone building became a symbol of the hierarchically organized Church with Christ as its head. The name *ecclesia* was rightly extended from the community of the faithful to the house of God. The basilica is over 100 yards long and more than 60 yards wide.

It is clear from a letter which Constantine wrote to the Bishop of Jerusalem that he wished churches founded by himself to excel all secular buildings in splendour and beauty. So coloured columns were taken from pagan buildings as spoils and trophies; they proclaimed the victory of the new religion and at the same time brought with them something of the dignity of the old.

According to not entirely reliable evidence from the eighth century, the walls of the nave bore a double row of pictures. They depicted the whole story of the redemption, from the expulsion of Adam from Eden to the reception of the good thief in paradise, in typological pairs of pictures from the Old and New Testaments. The flood was balanced by the baptism of Christ, Isaac with the bundle of wood by Christ with the cross, the passage through the Red Sea by the descent into hell, and the casting up of Jonas by the resurrection of Christ. The twelve apostles stood before the heavenly Jerusalem facing twelve prophets holding messianic texts.

Over the altar rose a finely embossed silver baldachin. On the front was a figure, 5 feet high, of Christ on his throne surrounded by the twelve apostles wearing crowns; on the back, Christ between four angels. In its four arches hung golden clusters of twenty lamps each, in the middle a gold chandelier of fifty lamps in the shape of dolphins. A still bigger chandelier hung in front of the baldachin. In the whole building Constantine set up one hundred and seventy-four candelabras with a total of more than eight thousand lamps, whose sparkling light produced an incomparable effect at nocturnal services.

Between 1646 and 1649 this venerable building—head and mother of all the Christian churches in the world—was transformed by Barromini, who converted each pair of columns into one massive pier, into a coldly splendid baroque ceremonial hall. The imposing façade was added by Alessandro Galilei in 1734.

ST PETER'S

The second, still more richly endowed church that Constantine built was the basilica of St Peter, on the slope of the Vatican hill, near Nero's Circus, over the spot where, according to tradition, Peter had been buried. This tradition must have been

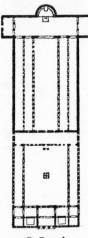

St Peter's

at that time quite undisputed, for the greatest difficulties were overcome in order to prepare the site for building. For a long time the ground up to Hadrian's mausoleum had been a cemetery. An avenue of tombs dating from the second and third centuries and containing the graves of some distinguished families was demolished. Only weighty reasons could have permitted this affront to piety. The site was very unfavourable, because the hill rose sharply from south to north, and less steeply from east to west. Large quantities of earth had to be moved and retaining walls had to be sunk 40 feet. The excavations under St Peter's made the development of the apostle's shrine up to

the time of Constantine quite clear. Under the confessio were found, at the lowest level, some graves of poor people which can be ascribed with certainty to the first century. A number of indications make it clear that this little area, and in particular one grave in the middle, was even then held in honour. In the second century pagan mausolea began to hem the site in dangerously, and it was protected on the north side by a wall about 9 feet high and 21 feet long, the so-called red wall, which runs over part of this grave. About A.D. 160 a shrine was built in front of a rounded niche in the wall which is continued in its foundation. This shrine consisted of two small pillars carrying a cross-piece about 6 feet by 2½. It is the tropaeum of which the presbyter Gaius wrote to the heretic

Proclus about 200, when the latter appealed to the graves of four prophetesses: "But I can point to the trophies—tropaea— of the apostles. For if you go to the Vatican, or along the road to Ostia, you will find the trophies of those who founded this church." Later on a crack appeared in the red wall and it was buttressed with a wall at right angles to it, to the right of the shrine; another was built on the left, and the whole was faced with slabs of marble. In Constantine's time it was already a

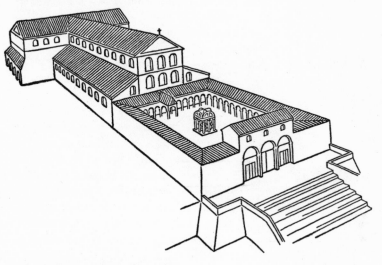

Old St Peter's. From the fourth century onwards there were two imperial mausolea and many oratories on the left. The atrium was later widened, and a tower and other buildings were added to the front wall.

venerable spot, covered with inscriptions of pilgrims; time had made it into one solid block, which it was felt undesirable to disturb, especially as there was an opening in the niche over the cross-piece through which votive offerings could be thrown down and small objects let down to touch the grave. The excavations have not solved all the problems, most of which arise out of the temporary removal of the bones to St Sebastian.

Nevertheless the results have been rich enough, for the continuous veneration of St Peter, which was linked to the place of burial, has been definitely associated with this spot under the present papal altar.

Constantine cased the memorial in marble and porphyry, put a ciborium on oriental pillars over it, and made it the centre of the new basilica. Behind a barrier of six pillars carved to look like twisting vine-tendrils, four of which formed a baldachin, the apostle's shrine stood in the finest spot in St Peter's, which

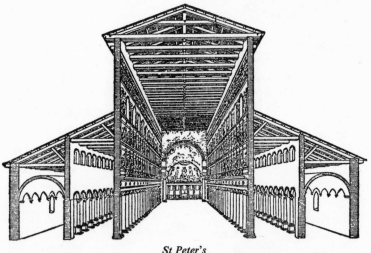

St Peter's

thus became itself a memorial church and the model for numerous churches dedicated to martyrs. We know more about it than about the church of the Redeemer, mainly through the canon and notary Giacomo Grimaldi, who made an exact record and somewhat less exact drawings of old St Peter's before it was demolished. The church measured 370 feet by 195 feet, and church and atrium together were nearly 700 feet long. At the end a broad line of steps similar to the present ones, divided into five flights of seven steps each, led up to the three

doors of the entrance building. Over the middle door was a
mosaic of Constantine thanking St Peter for recovery from a
serious illness. The end of the elegant inscription ran as follows:
"What a great honour Christ has conferred on Peter. The
former gave me life, the latter gave it back to me." The atrium
was a paradise garden, with evergreen trees, a vine and roses.
The big fountain in the middle was later replaced by the pine-
cone fountain, composed of valuable ancient pieces of stone. In
the cloister-like covered walk all round it distributions of alms
and meetings could take place. In the western cloister, which
opened into the basilica, the story of St Peter was depicted in
a cycle of twelve frescoes dating from somewhat later. There
were pictures of the collapse of the fleeing Simon Magus in
response to Peter's prayer, the *Quo vadis* scene, the conversion
of the Emperor Constantine and the crucifixion of the apostle.
Five entrances with bronze doors led into the basilica. It offered
a less unified, but no less splendid, picture than the Lateran
basilica, for various costly pillars and pieces of architecture
from older buildings had been employed. The lofty walls only
received their decoration in the time of Constantine's successor.
Over the flat entablature was a frieze of flowers in mosaic and
above that twenty-two scenes in fresco from the Old Testament
on the north wall, and the same number of scenes from the New
Testament on the south wall. The antithesis is based on the
idea that the Old Testament is the promise of the New, and the
New Testament the interpretation and fulfilment of the Old.
It soon became the rule, as is shown by the collection of *tituli*—
short verse explanations of pictures—in Paulinus of Nola and
Prudentius. Grimaldi's drawings suggest compositions full of
life and movement, which provided Raphael with the inspiration for some of his pictures.

Instead of Gothic windows we must visualize *transennae*, that
is, slabs of marble pierced in beautiful patterns, which let in,
like those in Santa Sabina today, a sufficiently bright, but not
harsh, light. Between the windows individual saints were

painted. According to an ancient description, the mosaic on the triumphal arch depicted, like the later one in St Paul's, the head and shoulders of Christ in a medallion, by his side full-length figures of St Peter and Constantine with a model of the church—the first founder's picture of this kind. The dedication ran as follows:

> *Quod Duce Te mundus surrexit in astra triumphans*
> *Hanc Constantinus Victor Tibi condidit aulam.*
> ("Because under thy leadership the world has risen triumphantly to heaven, Constantine the victor has dedicated this hall to thee.")

The very close link between the imperial protector and the church was emphasized a third time in the inscription on the mosaic in the apse. It praised the church as the dwelling of justice, faith and morality, Constantine and Constans as the virtuous founders of the Church. The mosaic was restored and somewhat altered under Innocent III. A faithful drawing of this version has been preserved. It showed Christ enthroned in glory against a background of golden stars, attested by the Father's hand holding the book of life, looking at and addressing the congregation. As representatives of the congregation, Peter and Paul do homage to him: "Thou art Christ, the son of the living God"; on their papyrus rolls is written "Christ is my life". At their feet children and animals play in a cheerful paradise landscape. Stags approach the four springs. In the lower strip twelve lambs are leaving the gates of Jerusalem and Bethlehem to join the Lamb on the mountain. Thus the transept was the real palace, the throne-room of Christ, the "image of the heavenly dwelling", in the words of Methodius of Olympus. The ceiling of St Peter's was painted with stars, like the imperial basilica on the Palatine, in which Septimius Severus presided over trials from the throne in the apse.

The church was very richly furnished. The silver altar-slab, which weighed 350 lb., was set with four hundred precious

stones and enclosed in a jewel-encrusted gold moulding. Over
the altar rose a gold baldachin. Curtains of precious material
between its pillars could veil the mystery of the transubstantia-
tion. A heavy golden chandelier, adorned with fifty dolphins,
hung in the middle, and four candelabras stood at the sides.
The church itself was illuminated by sixty-two silver candelabras and a number of chandeliers, which hung from the gilded
beams of the roof. One hundred lamps burnt continuously
round the confessio. In front of the altar the six twisted vine-
tendril pillars formed a kind of pergola, which was both barrier
and passage. One of these pillars now stands in the chapel of
the Pietà; Bernini placed the others by the central columns of
the new St Peter's, using them as models for the twisted bronze
pillars of the tabernacle under the dome. The papal cathedra
stood in the apse, surrounded by the marble seats of the
presbyters. The semicircular wall was faced with sheets of gold
up to the point where the mosaics began. In the course of time
the roof acquired gilded bronze tiles, and the front wall over
the atrium-cloister a mosaic of the adoration of the Lamb.
The land round the church long remained a cemetery containing both pagan and Christian mausolea. On the south side there
stood for a long time several altars of the Magna Mater, a
mother-goddess much revered in late antiquity. In the fourth
century imperial tombs were erected in the south transept.
Round the great church there soon grew up a jumble of little
churches, hospices and palaces, as we know from medieval
drawings.

In the first centuries the sacrifice of the Mass could not be
celebrated over the apostle's grave, but only in front of it. In
the long run this caused more and more sadness, especially as
in many other memorial churches grave and altar were identical.
Developments tended in this direction. An edict of 787 laid
down that every altar had to contain the relics of a martyr.
Gregory the Great undertook the conversion, which can still be
seen in Raphael's picture of Constantine's bequest. He had the

level of the ground raised, except at the front, so that only the upper part of the ciborium was visible and could be made into an altar. Now it was possible to celebrate Mass *over* the apostle's grave, as it says in the old papal book. The pillars of

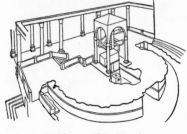

the baldachin were moved forward so as to form a row. When the ground was raised, a circular passage was left round the wall of the apse, with a branch to the confessio. Small groups of pilgrims could now stop at the grave, and large parties could be led past

Confessio of St Peter's

without a halt. When the new St Peter's was built in the sixteenth century, the whole floor of the old church was raised by one storey—the so-called grottos. In front of the confessio, there remained a depression which preserved something of the impression of the earlier layout and left free the barrier opening to the apostle's grave.

The new papal altar, crowned by Bernini's baldachin, was erected over the old one.

ST PAUL'S

The third big basilica with a transept was founded by the emperor in 386 in place of a small church over the apostle's grave on the road to Ostia. After the fire of 1823 it was rebuilt according to the old measurements, so that here alone it is still possible to gain some idea of the majesty of the imperial basilicas. Seven doors open out of the square atrium into the four-aisled nave. The inner arcades are somewhat taller than the outer ones; they are also of more sumptuous material and workmanship. The apostle's grave lies behind the triumphal arch, which was spared by the fire, in the wide, deep transept.

The mosaics were not completed until the middle of the fifth century. The triumphal arch is dominated by the head and shoulders of Christ, wearing the crown of glory, and surrounded by the twenty-four worshipping elders and the four creatures of the Apocalypse. Over the arcades was a line of medallions of the popes, and above that a double row of pictures from the Old and New Testaments. Between the windows there were prophets and saints.

PARISH CHURCHES

The initiative and generosity of the emperor, together with the talent and culture of his architects, gave Christian architecture in the first half of the fourth century a remarkably unified character. The influence of these buildings made itself felt in the smaller ones erected in the next hundred years by the Church itself, that is, the popes. Parish churches were usually built as three-aisled basilicas without a transept; the apse spanned the whole width of the central nave. The forty private churches attributed by Optatus of Mileve to pre-Constantine Rome were for the most part replaced by public buildings; they retained their old, respected names.

SANTA SABINA

Santa Sabina on the Aventine, built in the time of Celestine I (422–32), is the best preserved parish church of this early period. It reveals more of the spirit of the primitive Church than the big buildings do: remoteness from the world, sense of the one thing necessary, brotherly community, and expectation of the second coming of Christ. It is very significant that the eschatological mood of the early Church grew more spiritual, not weaker, as it settled down in the world. It recognized that the return of the Lord is not only the terminal point of history but also the deepest meaning of life on earth now.

Santa Sabina gives a tremendous impression of light. All round it there is a tall line of big round-arched windows: three in the apse, three in the back wall and twelve on each side above the twelve shadowy arcades of the ground floor. Below, enough light gets into the narrow, once windowless side-aisles to unify the whole space, but the contrast remains strong enough to make the upper part of the building give the impression of heaven, and the lower part that of sure protection from the storms of life on earth: house of God, flooded by light from above, house of the community, which has fled for safety into the fold of the Lord and huddles like one big family round the rails of the sanctuary. It is an ideal place for the celebration of the liturgy, which puts before us at the same time the earthly death and heavenly glorification of the Lord. Most of the mosaics have been lost. On the entrance-wall, beside the consecration-inscription, are two female figures, the Jewish Church and the gentile Church; over these, beside the windows, are Peter and Paul, and right at the top the four creatures of the Apocalypse. It is the Church militant seen from an eschatological point of view. Its homage joins that of the fourteen apostles and evangelists, whose portraits flank the great bust of Christ in the front of the Church on the arch of the apse. The mosaics on the side-walls probably showed the historical work of redemption, while the mosaic on the apse combined temporal and eternal in one powerful symbol (see illustration 15).

SANTA MARIA MAGGIORE

Shortly after the completion of Santa Sabina, Pope Sixtus III (432–40) rebuilt the church of Our Lady originally put up in the time of Liberius. After the Council of Ephesus had proclaimed the honour due to Mary as the Mother of God, he wanted to give the city a shrine dedicated to Mary that could take its place by the side of the three imperial basilicas. As in St Peter's and many other Roman churches, the entrance is at the east end. The central nave is 50 feet wide and over 210 feet long. The twenty Ionic columns on each side carry, instead of arches, a straight, moulded architrave, as in the old St Peter's. Raised mouldings rise between the windows and form the fields for the mosaics. It is a peaceful, solemn building, far more reminiscent than Santa Sabina of classical architecture. Originally the nave ended immediately behind the triumphal arch in the apse; the transept was added later. So the main picture of this church, whose mosaics are otherwise the most completely preserved we have, has unfortunately disappeared. We should very much like to know if here Mary was to be seen—for the first time— by the side of Christ. In any case, in the existing mosaic on the triumphal arch the usual picture of the second coming is very much diminished in size and broken up. In the middle, over Sixtus' dedicatory inscription,

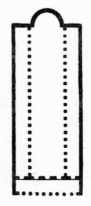

Santa Maria Maggiore

we see, between Peter, Paul and the four living creatures, a blue halo with the throne. On this is the jewelled cross, diadem and mantle of Christ. On the footstool is the papyrus roll with the seven seals. From below, where the round arch begins, twelve lambs look up longingly from the holy cities of Jerusalem and Bethlehem to the halo. In between, in three zones, there are scenes, based on the gospel of the pseudo-Matthew and in the style of the court ceremonial pictures, emphasizing the royal dignity of the Madonna and her child. Wearing a diadem and surrounded by angels, she sits listening to the Annunciation. Joseph, depicted as a vigorous husband, is released from his uncertainty by an angel. To the right of the halo is the presentation in the temple of the goddess Rome, as the figure of Rome in the pediment shows. All the hopes of the renewal of the empire which were bound up with this shrine have been fulfilled by Christ in a higher sense. In the middle strip on the left is depicted the adoration of the Magi. Beside the throne of the little King sits Mary as a royal princess and also another woman, perhaps the gentile Church. Behind the throne is the bodyguard of angels and the star, the sign of the new-born King. On the right is the arrival in Egypt. An apocryphal legend tells how at the appearance of Christ the statues of the gods crashed to the ground and the governor Aphrodisius came hurrying up with his troops, but was converted by the miracle. This story, too, has been completely remodelled to fit in with the idea of Christ the Emperor. It is the solemn welcome which the governor and the citizens of a provincial town accord to the emperor. The lower strip shows the vain exertions of the enemies of God, the dealings of Herod with the Magi and the murder of the Holy Innocents. The symbol of the throne at the top unifies the whole: King of Kings, Lord of Lords.

These pictures already show the solemn, restrained style which developed in the fifth and sixth centuries and which is so well adapted to the portrayal of the supernatural world. Blue, gold, white and red are the basic colours. The mosaics in the nave, on the other hand, with their fresh green, yellow and red, give a Hellenistic effect. Wilpert ascribed them with good reason to Liberius' fourth-century basilica, but more recent investigators put them in the fifth century. The riddle of the differences in style is explained by the fact that the mosaics of the nave, like the pictures of Dura-Europos, to which they are related, go back to early pictorial compositions of the Hellenistic Diaspora. They begin near the altar with scenes from the Old Testament which bear some relation to the sacrifice of the New Testament—the sacrifice of Melchisedech, the meal of the three men with Abraham—and then tell in more and more lively fashion the story of Abraham, Isaac and Jacob on the left-hand side, and the story of Moses and Josue on the right-hand side.

The basilica with three naves remained the rule at Rome for

many centuries. In the rebuilding of San Lorenzo (579–90) and in the construction of Santa Agnese (625–30) the conception was enriched in imitation of East Roman models, by raising the height without abandoning the tall clerestory. None of the wonderful central spaces of the East was taken over as the space for the congregation; the only exception is Santo Stefano Rotondo, which was remodelled from an older building with stronger emphasis of the axis into one of the most beautiful of interiors (468–83). In the next few centuries Christian art at Rome did not decay, but it found no great tasks to undertake. The existing churches sufficed for the reduced population. They were furnished with a wealth of paintings. They are limpid, artless votive pictures, often Madonnas of homely sublimity, with pious founders. In a former library in the Forum, the little church of Santa Maria Antiqua was discovered, covered all over with pictures dating from the sixth to the ninth century; in places there were several layers on top of each other.

In the ninth century they began to build churches again in Rome, but without any creative development. Among others arose San Martino ai Monti, Quattro Coronati and Santa Maria in Domnica, with its wonderful picture in the apse of the Madonna between groups of angels (see illustration 44). Noteworthy is the echo of early wealthy buildings in the cruciform basilicas of San Stefano Maggiore and San Prassede, with their rich mosaics. They are followed later by Santa Maria in Trastevere, San Crisogono and Ara Coeli.

The Roman basilica did not become the universal norm for Italy. In Milan, the new capital of the western empire, as early as 400, models from Asia Minor were preferred to the Roman ones. They are influenced by the cult of martyrs and must be discussed in this new connection.

In Syria and Palestine in the fourth and fifth centuries the basilica underwent its most important alterations, which were to be of great importance for western architecture as well.

These two countries were at that time artistically the richest in Christendom. Palestine is said to have possessed a thousand churches. Antioch was a patriarchate with over two hundred bishoprics. There were about a hundred townships and villages in the neighbourhood of the city, and even the smaller ones often had four or five churches.

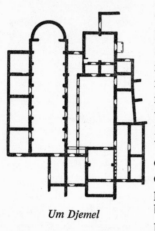

That gives us some idea of all that has perished in the metropolis itself. Syria was always a buffer state, but it was strong enough to preserve its individuality. Under the Seleucids its political and cultural ties were with Mesopotamia, under the Romans it became a part of the West with its unified Hellenic culture. Baalbek and Palmyra are evidence of this, and also the imperial palace at Spalato, modelled by a Syrian architect on the island palace at Antioch.

Um Djemel

The presence of good limestone facilitated at an early date the construction of stone churches, long single-naved buildings with a semicircular apse such as the church of Julianos at Um Djemel, which dates from 345. The ceiling consists of plinthed arches with stone beams resting on them. Even these single-naved basilicas sometimes possess two rooms behind the apse, called pastophoria: the prothesis as a room for the table with the bread and wine, and the diakonikon as a room for the deacons, vessels and vestments. Two side apses were introduced, even in hall-churches. The triple-naved, pillared basilica holds its ground, especially in northern Syria. In other areas, especially the Haman, which is poor in wood, pillared basilicas of very different kinds were built. In accordance with pre-Christian tradition, galleried churches without a clerestory arose. Plinthed arches cross the short space in closely-spaced rows and are continued in smaller arches above the gallery. The floors of

the galleries and the roof consist of stone beams. The ruins of
Jaffa still convey some idea of these heavy, dark churches.
Where there was wood, the arches could be put further apart.
This was the case in the church of the Apostles at I'dschas at

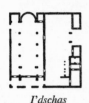

I'dschas

the beginning of the fifth century. You can
see on the ground plan the narthex (vestibule)
in the west, the wide arches of the nave and
the triple bema at the west end. The atrium
adjoins the south side and has become a
living-space with rooms and halls. Probably
we have here a conception derived from the
synagogue and passed on to the western monastery, that is, the
dwelling for monks round the cloister on the south side of the
church.

At Serdschilla the church broadens out before the tripartite
sanctuary into a kind of transept. The building is enclosed on
the long sides by colonnades (sixth century).

Gradually the intervals
between the pillars grow
greater and greater.
Finally the whole space is
intersected by no more
than three deep arches. It
is divided by these
three transverse
arches into three
clear sections, but
also bound again
into one contin-
uous space by
the longitudinal

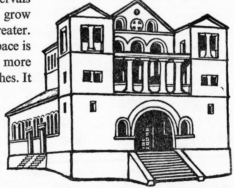

Turmanin

beams of the roof. As a result of the big openings, the side-
aisles are united much more closely to the main central area.
The pillars are flanked by half-columns. In the clerestory small
pillars on bases carry the beams. Portals and round-arched

windows are framed by raised mouldings. The doors in the long sides have no porches. The apse is frequently drawn into the main area and enclosed, together with the pastophoria, in a perpendicular outside wall. The portico is flanked by tower-shaped outbuildings. Turmanin, which dates from about 500, has a façade of this sort with two towers; in front of the richly decorated gable there is an open portico. Luzeh lacks the colonnade over the entrance and the second storey of the towers, but here on the other hand the projecting apse and tall pastophoria acquire the status of a façade. If today we particularly value the Romanesque style for its austere strength, nothing in early Christian art will seem so familiar as these Syrian churches, straightforwardly and strongly constructed as they are out of accurately cut blocks of stone. In fact, when they were discovered a hundred years ago by the Marquis de Vogué, their direct influence on the West was recognized at once (see illustration 28).

At Edessa, the centre of the kingdom of Osroene, there is evidence of the existence of churches as early as the second century. Some time after 200 the royal family was converted to Christianity. By 300 there were twenty-five churches in Edessa; we know their names. We do not know precisely what any of them looked like. According to written tradition the pillared basilica was the prevailing style. But the ruins of the basilica of Sergius at Rusafa on the Euphrates, which date from the sixth century, display considerable similarity to the church of Bizzos at Ruhweha, which was built about 500. The main difference is that it is built on a grander scale. Wide arches resting on piers span elegant pillared arcades. The tower, too, betrays the relationship to the Syrian churches.

Mesopotamian churches were modelled on the native temples and palaces. A long barrel-vault rests on low pillars arranged in pairs, but the niches and cross-vaults between them do not link up to form side-aisles. The building ends in the tripartite sanctuary. A church in Kilisse el-Ahmar near Kirkuk

—it dates from the sixth or seventh century—can serve as an example. In order to secure a closer connection with the altar, the barrel-vaulted nave is often arranged sideways.

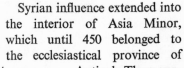

Syrian influence extended into the interior of Asia Minor, which until 450 belonged to the ecclesiastical province of Antioch. The mountain range of the Kara Dagh alone preserves in the monastery town of Bimbir-Kilisse (the town of 1001 churches) the ruins of sixteen churches.

Rusafa

Like the Syrian churches, they possess freestone façades with two towers, but of a simple, shallower kind. The nave is covered with a plaster barrel-vault running lengthways; the aisles sometimes have transverse barrel-vaults. The square piers are often strengthened with pillars or half-pillars. Pastophoria do not often occur. If there are galleries, the nave is not raised very much; the result is dimly lit churches that give an impression of massive weight.

The Syrian liturgy was responsible for another

Bimbir-Kilisse

peculiarity which can be observed in many churches. There is a kind of second sanctuary in the middle of the nave.

Balustrades enclosed a raised rectangular area whose western
end was semicircular in form. It was entered from the east
through a door which led through the high, broad lectorium
or pulpit. The surrounding bench ended in the semicircle at the
etimasia, the throne for the gospel-book and later for the
bishop, too. This bema was used for the office of the martyr,
the reading and sermon. In Nestorian churches there was an
altar in the middle with a baldachin. At Rusafa the whole
precinct was covered over.

Syrian churches influenced early church architecture in
Dalmatia, Istria and Ravenna.

AFRICA

In size, Alexandria was the second city of the ancient world;
in culture, the first. It was one of the big metropoles of the early
Church. One hundred and ten bishoprics were subject to it. Its
early churches have vanished without trace. All we can do is to
draw vague conclusions about the art of the capital from the
churches of the hinterland. The White and Red monasteries in
the Thebais, which date from the first half of the fifth century,
both possessed clover-shaped apses with superimposed rows of
pillars. The apses were preceded by a broad transept. The naves
had galleries. They were Hellenistic buildings of a highly
developed kind. In the nearby town of Mena alone four pillared
basilicas that differ from each other have been uncovered.
Typical of Egyptian buildings and those they influenced in
North Africa are the multiplication of the naves to five, seven
or even nine, the triple apse and the quite frequently occurring
counter-apse at the west end, a feature owing its origin to the
cult of the saints.

North Africa with its capital, Carthage, was long one of the
most prosperous provinces of the early Church. About 250,
ninety bishops met in Lambesa. K. M. Kaufmann points to an
endless list of destroyed churches. No excavation in Africa is

Hippo

more interesting than the one conducted by the former naval officer Erwan Marec on the open space once occupied by Hippo. He sought and found the little theocracy where St Augustine lived in brotherly community with his friends and strengthened his fellow bishops in the struggle against heresy. He found the church in which the saint addressed his congregation so charmingly, and the consignatorium in which he impressed on the candidate for confirmation the greatness of being a Christian. Several houses of an older block were purchased in the fourth century from pagan owners—this is shown by the themes of the

Hippo

splendid mosaic floor—and made into a Christian block. The church was built on the foundation of a bigger building and opened straight on to the street; there was no atrium. It was a three-aisled, pillared basilica. Round the apse it had the stone bench for the clergy with the bishop's throne in the middle, a raised altar area that projected into the nave and was enclosed by a balustrade, and in front of it, stretching almost right across the central nave, a burial vault, in which St Augustine was probably buried, too. Opening out of the right-hand aisle was a fairly big chapel. On one side it led to the rectangular room for the catechumens, and from there to the roughly circular baptistery. The font has been preserved; it is 3 feet deep and once had a baldachin over it. On the other side of the chapel were rooms for changing clothes and washing, for the neophytes had to be immaculate when they came to be baptized. As at Tipara, Timgad and Fréjus, all these rooms concerned with baptism were built in a former public bath.

To the east lay the dwellings of the monastic community. They surrounded the apse and left space on the north side for a little paradise garden. To the left of the entrance to the church were probably the bishop's offices. Adjoining these were guest-rooms, a chapel with three apses and a spacious colonnaded court. Here meetings took place. The extreme left-hand corner contained the domestic offices.

On the other side of the street which skirts the whole precinct, Marec uncovered, on the right-hand side, the foundations of a church with five aisles.

ABYSSINIA

Abyssinia with its capital Aksum, which was founded by Arabs, was converted to Christianity by Syrian monks in the fourth century, and was known thereafter as Ethiopia. Its nine bishops were subject to Alexandria. In the fifth century it became Monophysite, like Armenia and part of Syria. Since the seventh century Arab Christians have been known as Copts. In contrast to Alexandria they developed a strongly individual liturgy and art based on popular tradition. They built numerous basilicas, probably because of their spaciousness, among them the chief church at Aksum which has five aisles, but for smaller parish and monastery churches they clung to their native style of architecture, which had developed almost the same kind of building for temples, palaces and tombs. Coptic churches seem to consist of rectangular towers of two storeys. They are reminiscent of Babylonian buildings. The interior is divided by a short row of pillars. The sanctuary is tripartite and ends in an ordinary straight wall. Smaller churches often have an altar area enclosed by walls in the middle of the nave. The church as a whole is surrounded by a courtyard containing graves and living quarters for the priests. The monastery church of Debra Damo, which is on a tall rock, will serve as an example. More

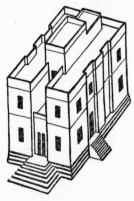

Debra Damo

important are the book-illustrations and sculpture of the Copts, which influenced the West through the Lombards and Celts. The carving in relief of Christ riding a horse shows how they disdained both natural forms and Alexandrian beauty, and were thereby enabled to get all the closer to spiritual reality (see illustration 36).

BYZANTIUM

In the fifth century Byzantium was still only one centre among many, receiving as well as giving. It was not until the sixth century that its imperial style submerged all others. Byzantium took over the Roman basilica and enriched it with many characteristics which had developed in the coastal towns of Asia Minor. The basilica of Menas, for example, erected by the Emperor Arcadius about 400, has affinities with the martyrium of John in Ephesus. The basilica of Demetrius in Salonica, built in the fifth century, had a similar ground-plan.

It was destroyed by fire in 1917, but carefully rebuilt. Roman strictness is here considerably relaxed. There are no smooth walls to force one's gaze down the nave to the altar. The interior is transformed by brightly lit side-aisles and galleries into a broad, festive hall. Above the galleries the stout walls are pierced a third time by numerous low windows. They thus become sculptured structures of great power. The alternation in supports—one pier to every four columns—strengthens this impression and articulates the space, but it was probably not devised until the rebuilding in the seventh century. The apse has five big windows and is thus on the way to becoming an illuminated choir.

The oldest remaining basilica in Constantinople, the church of St John, in the monastery founded by the patrician Studios in 463, is a very un-Roman building. The ground-plan is nearly a square. The way up to the altar is shortened to an arcade of eight arches. The central space is only twice as long as it is broad, and it is divided still further by the galleries. Under Persian influence, the decoration is beginning to play a more and more important part in the general effect. Green pillars support white capitals and architraves. The walls were covered with a layer of white marble which was once coloured, and the floor had a mosaic pattern made out of brightly coloured pieces of marble, richly interspersed with flowers and animals. It is no longer a processional church in the earlier sense, but an attempt at a central space, a concept which achieved greater success by a different path. This single remaining example must not be used to justify general conclusions. If eighty years later splendid basilicas were still being built in Ravenna under Byzantine influence, this venerable form cannot have been neglected in the East. And in fact Justinian built the new church of Mary in Jerusalem, the Nea, with its big porches and semi-circular projecting atrium, as a galleried basilica as splendid as Constantine's buildings. The greatest achievement of Byzantine art lay in the creation of the church with a big central area.

TEMPLES AND SYNAGOGUES

When, in the fourth century, the Christians celebrated their victory and drove the heathens from the most influential positions into the country—henceforth they are known as pagans, that is, villagers—there were still four hundred splendid temples in Rome. What happened to them? The historian of art puts this question with feelings rather different from those of the ecclesiastical historian. The attitude of the Christians varied enormously from place to place and from period to period. It was not until 356 that an imperial decree ordered the closing of the temples. Temple property fell to the State, but the Church was allocated a proportion of it. In the East temples were at first destroyed; in the West there was a decree about A.D. 400 protecting them. A law of 435 ordered the closing, desecration and, in certain cases, destruction of temples.

Gregory the Great advised the Anglo-Saxons to christianize rather than destroy temples. In this case only the altar and the image of the god were destroyed. High artistic value was often a ground for preserving images. Constantinople was richly adorned with works of this kind from all over the Roman world. In Greece, Asia Minor and Sicily the classical temples were converted into churches by additions or alterations. The Parthenon at Athens became a three-aisled basilica, and the Theseum a church with one nave. The pillars round the outside remained as they were. In Syracuse they were joined by a wall, and the cella inside was enlarged by the removal and piercing of walls into a multi-aisled hall. The result was by no means a Christian church, for every visible part of the temple shows how immune it was to the mixture. In Syria and Palestine the whole temple was frequently pulled down and the stones used to build a church on the same foundations. Often, and always in Egypt, the inner sanctuary of the temple was avoided and the church built in a portico. It was seldom that a temple was taken over without alterations, but this did happen with the Pantheon, which became a church dedicated to Mary in the sixth century. In such cases the heathen pictures and reliefs were always torn out and the walls prepared for Christian pictures.

Synagogues, too, were often christianized. In the Gelasian Sacramentary there is a special ritual for this. In 535 Justinian ordered the conversion of all African synagogues into churches. Sometimes only the outside walls were retained. The interior was often radically altered, orientated and enlarged by the addition of an apse.

Secular buildings were only converted into churches for special reasons and with fundamental alterations. Thus a big room in the Sessorian palace, in which the Empress-mother Helena lived, was transformed by the addition of the apse and other alterations into the "Church of the Holy Cross at Jerusalem", to honour the relic of the Cross.

CHAPTER III

THE MARTYRIUM

The basilica, as a link between congregation and sanctuary, a pilgrim's path to eternity, must have corresponded perfectly to the Roman Church with its hierarchical organization and clear, objective liturgy, for it remained unaltered for many centuries. It served extremely well for the celebration of the sacrifice, less well for adoration. Only a vaulted space can represent heaven over the earth; only a central space can express the peace of a goal achieved and of rest in God. Because here on earth there can be no final discovery of God, the ideal Christian building is not a perfectly round church after the pattern of the Pantheon, which suggests the apotheosis of cosmic forces, but a combination of central space and length, in which movement and rest, seeking and finding are expressed simultaneously. The East strove harder than the West after this ideal form. One of the many reasons for this was the divergence in liturgy and devotion which emerged after the fourth century. At this time the eastern Churches began to develop their mystical and emotional liturgies of adoration. In the struggle against Arius, who saw in Christ only the first creation of the Father, less emphasis was placed on Christ the mediator than on his essentially equivalent divinity. Prayers were no longer addressed to the Father "through Christ in the Holy Spirit", but directly to the Father "and the Son together with the Holy Spirit". The angels and saints gained increased significance as mediators if—in Chrysostom's words—"the

holy, awe-inspiring, dreadful secrets" were celebrated and the
King of Kings appeared. The Mass certainly remained a
redemptive sacrifice, but it was felt more strongly as a solemn
act of adoration. Such an attitude demanded churches that
could be more directly copies of heaven. So the East did not
remain satisfied with the very functional basilicas erected everywhere by Constantine, but altered the basilica in the direction
of the building with a larger central space. It happened very
conveniently that from the start, beside the basilica-type
churches for community worship, there also existed buildings
focused for various purposes on a central space: mausolea,
baptisteries and martyria, that is, places of witness. Of these
the martyrium is by far the most important.

MAUSOLEA

In accordance with ancient royal custom, several tombs were
erected in the fourth century for the imperial family. The
mausoleum of the Empress Helena, planned originally in all
probability for Constantine, directly adjoined the nave of the
church of St Peter and St Marcellus. The impressive ruins of the
so-called Pignatarra Gate still give some idea of this rotunda.
It was a cylinder 60 feet in diameter and 45 feet high, roofed
over by a semicircular dome. The walls are about 12 feet thick,
and have niches hollowed out in them, alternately rectangular
and round. The biggest niche, the one in the east, was to receive
the sarcophagus of the empress.

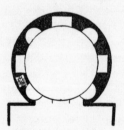

Mausoleum of Helena

Constantine had his own mausoleum
built in the new capital as the apse of
the church of the Apostles. Between the
pillars of the colonnade were twelve
sarcophagi representing symbolically
the tombs of the apostles. He wished
to be buried himself in his porphyry
sarcophagus in their midst behind

the altar, as "the apostles' equal", the representative of Christ.

Two hundred years later the Merovingian King Sigismund had a similar mausoleum built for himself and his family in the apse of St Peter's at Geneva.

ST COSTANZA

Well preserved and still fascinating is the mausoleum (or baptistery) of Constantine's daughter Constantia, quite unjustifiably known as St Costanza. A barrel-vaulted colonnade with sixteen niches stands round the brightly lit central space like a dark backing. Twelve arcades borne by double columns with tall entablatures form the link between the two. The walls were covered with marble, while the vaults and floor

St Costanza

were adorned with mosaics. Only those in the colonnade and some of the niches have been preserved. Those in the colonnade display bright patterns on a white ground, with a wealth of little motifs—such as the wine-harvest, cupids, dolphins and birds—suggesting the landscape of paradise. In one side-niche there is a picture of Christ in a yellow robe standing like a ruler over the four rivers of paradise between four lambs, handing over the Law to Peter to the applause of Paul. In the other niche a bearded Christ is enthroned, with a halo, on the globe of the earth, handing the keys to Peter. Dominating these scenes was a picture of the heavenly Jerusalem in the light-shaft of the niche opposite the entrance. Here stood the porphyry sarcophagus in the Vatican museum, which, with all its heavy vine-tendrils and cherubs picking grapes, repeated the motifs of the colonnade. The tambour displayed a mixture of pagan and Christian symbols of immortality. In an idyllic river

Salonica

landscape there were birds, and a boat ferrying the dead over to the next world. Above this, heavy tendrils like candelabras divided the lower part of the dome into twelve fields; these and the dome itself were adorned with biblical scenes on a blue ground. The baroque age had little understanding for decorative art of this sort in the service of architecture; it destroyed the mosaics and obscured the wonderfully bright interior with paintings intended to convey the illusion of space.

The mausoleum of Diocletian at Spalato and the huge funerary rotunda of Galerius at Salonica were later converted into splendid churches by the addition of small apses and mosaic decorations.

BAPTISTERIES

The importance of baptism as the sacrament of entry into the Church and the practice of administering it by immersion led, as early as the third century, to the provision of special rooms for baptism next to the house-churches. After 313 they were built as small centralized buildings by the side of parish and diocesan churches. In form, they were modelled either on mausolea—baptism is burial with Christ and resurrection to a new life—or on Roman baths, especially the *frigidaria*, or cold-water rooms. Constantine's baptistery in the Lateran basilica resembled in ground-plan the *frigidarium* at Pompeii.

In Italy, baptisteries are usually round or octagonal buildings with niches and a clerestory, a vaulted or flat roof, and arcades or a colonnade. The finest example of this kind is at Nocera near Salerno. It was built separately from St Costanza, but is intimately connected with it by the fact that its vault begins directly over the arcades of the colonnade. The interior of the Lateran baptistery was built by Sixtus III (432–40). Eight pillars carry the upper walls and the dome; the central space in the middle is completely filled by the font. This plan was very frequently imitated, for example at Riez, where corner niches have been added. Three- or four-apsed buildings were also numerous. Foundations uncovered at Nevers show how artistically these little structures were planned.

In Africa, the square or rectangular form was often chosen; the baldachin over the font was also square. In Syria a miniature copy of a basilica was adopted, a rectangle or square with an apse; it was often completely occupied by the font and divided from the rest of the building by a balustrade.

An example of mosaic decoration has been partly preserved in the baptistery at Naples, which dates from the second half of the fourth century. At the apex is the monogram of Christ, and in the eight sectors below the appointment of Peter as Christ's successor, the saving of Peter from the water, the miraculous draught of fishes, the promise of the

Riez

water of life to the Samaritan woman and the changing of the water into wine. On the walls are the symbols of the evangelists.

MARTYRIA

The pagan world had developed little memorial buildings for the cult of heroes. They were called *heroa*, and were vaulted centralized buildings on a square, octagonal, round, clover-leaf or cruciform foundation. Even the round ones usually had four niches inside arranged in the shape of a cross. After the Edict of Toleration these memorials were taken over for the cult of the Christian heroes, the martyrs. Even in the age of persecution, those who had testified with their blood were honoured on the anniversary of their death, their *dies natalis*, the day of birth into eternal life, by the celebration of the Mass at their tombs. But it was only in the retrospect of the fourth century, in the joy at the victory which the martyrs had bought with their blood, that the veneration of the saints gained its great importance in popular devotion, the liturgy and art. People visited their graves. Pilgrimages started. As the removal of the bones was still forbidden, shrines were built on the actual site of the martyrdom, where God had asserted himself as the martyrs' strength. As martyrs became scarce in the fourth century, witnesses were granted equal honour, because they were ready for the same sacrifice. "Implevit sine cruore martyrium", "he accomplished a bloodless martyrdom", says Sulpicius Severus of St Martin of Tours. "A fine life before God is a constant martyrdom", says Jerome, speaking of virgins. At this period, the body of a saint was, to an extent that it is difficult for us to imagine, a valuable treasure and an effective protection, which warded off enemies and averted catastrophes. The cult of saints was usually linked to the cult of their relics. St John Chrysostom

St Gereon, Cologne

explains the reason for this, a reason that was still in the forefront of men's minds in the Middle Ages: the bodies of the saints, who lived in Christ and were dead to the world, were members of Christ and temples of the Holy Ghost. For this reason they are rightly put in the altar on which Christ appears and venerated with him. The first removal of relics, that of St Babylas, took place at Antioch in 354. They soon became quite frequent, especially at Byzantium, which did not wish to be left behind by the other metropoles. In 357 St Timothy was taken there, and soon afterwards St Andrew and St Luke. In the fourth century, too, the division of bodies began. "Grace remains entire with every part", says Theodoretus. In the West removal was still forbidden. An edict of Theodosius allows, at the most, whole sarcophagi to be moved. But the barbarian invasions necessitated the transference of the bones of the martyrs to safer cities. In such cases, however, veneration at the spot where they had given their lives did not cease.

Martyria were rectangular, round, triple-apsed or cruciform; they were to be found in great numbers outside towns, inside them and in monasteries. The long list of the churches of Ravenna must have referred in the main to these small buildings. The vast majority of them have perished. A building with three apses still stands over the catacomb of St Callisto. The foundations of rectangular martyria were discovered under the Minster in Bonn and at Xanten. St Gereon at Cologne, a full-sized church, was built some time before 400; it is oval in shape with ten niches, following the pattern of the centralized buildings of Constantine's time. The oldest church

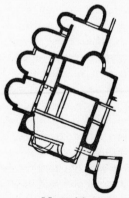

Manastirine

in Germany to the east of the Rhine was built in 706 in the fortress of Marienberg at Würzburg; it is a vaulted rotunda with eight niches, like an early Christian martyrium. Because the martyria were too small, a normal basilica was frequently

St Pierre-le-Vif, Sens

built as a memorial over the grave of a martyr. Rome became the holy city because a ring of such martyria rose outside its walls. Some of the most famous— apart from the basilicas of the apostles— are St Laurence, St Valentine and St Pancras. They were built with a deep-set floor, so that the altar was as close as possible to the grave. A small opening in the altar-stone, known as the fenestella, provided a direct link with the tomb. But pilgrims wanted more, so it became the custom to build a circular crypt round the wall of the apse, as at St Peter's, with an entrance to the tomb in the middle. If the founders or others wished to be buried near the saint, the crypt was enlarged. The choir would then be raised several steps. It can often only be reached by stairs at the sides, because in the middle steps lead straight down to the vault. Round the vault were built chapels radiating outwards for altars or further graves. Thus the deep-set martyr's grave, a martyrium inside the church, noticeably changed the church interior. It was not until the Gothic period that crypts became superfluous, when the bones of the saints were put on the altar in golden caskets.

A second possibility consisted in connecting martyria and parish-churches together. This produced, round many big buildings, charming cloisters of memorial chapels grouped in no particular order. They were often built on to the nave instead of the apse, in order to make access to them easier. In the case of new churches, built in honour of a famous saint, an organic connection was preferred.

One of the first Roman memorial churches is a good example.

It is the basilica of the Apostles on the Appian Way, in the depressions—*ad catacumbas*, hence the term catacombs—the one that later took its name from St Sebastian, who had been buried here in the time of Diocletian.

The princes of the apostles had long been venerated here, because they were buried here for a time, in a martyrium with a triclia, a room for the funeral meal, adjoining it. Round

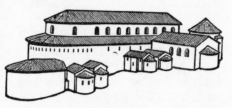

St Sebastian

this central point the catacomb spread out further and further. In Constantine's time the whole area was covered up and a memorial church built on the top of it. The building was primarily a nave, for it was to serve as a parish church, but the recollection that this was a site of witness transformed the basilica into a martyr's shrine. It started at the east end with an atrium and narthex and ended in a semicircle which the lengthened side-aisles enclosed like a processional way. Thus a halved funerary rotunda coalesced with the nave of a basilica to form a new unified building over 200 feet long and over 90 feet wide. Its supports were not columns but square piers. This austere and dignified building was also regarded as a cemetery. There were soon rows of arcosolia along the side-walls, graves in the floor and small mausolea outside. The first church of St Agnes on the Via Nomentana was very similar; its earth-filled retaining walls today contain a garden.

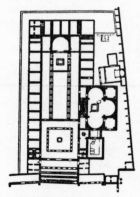

Tebessa in Africa

In the basilica of Felix at Nola a triple-apsed martyrium was combined with the usual long nave. An early church on the site of Mainz cathedral seems to have followed the same plan. Every possible combination was tried out in this period. In Gaul the basilica was sometimes left as it was and a rotunda built on to the apse at the east end.

The largest complex of buildings—it can only be compared with that of Jerusalem—was in the imperial city of Trier. Where the present cathedral and church of Our Lady stand, a double church was built on the foundation of an imperial palace. The work began in 326. At Aquileia there were two basilicas with a baptistery in between. The northern one was altered in 340, and the apse was replaced by a polygonal layout like that of the church of the Nativity at Bethlehem. It may well have been a shrine devoted to Christ, as the one at Bethlehem was, for the preservation of relics and cloths which had come into contact with the holy places of Palestine—cloth-relics, as they were called.

The degree of veneration accorded to them may be judged from the fact that in the time of the Emperor Gratian, near the end of the fourth century, the dodecagonal shrine was encased

Trier

in the square choir which can still be distinguished as a large block in the present cathedral. At that time the Apocalypse exerted considerable influence on sarcophagi, mosaics and small works of art, and the intention here may well have been to create for once a large-scale reproduction of the city of God. "The city lies foursquare, the same in its length as its breadth. . . . The fashioning of its walls was of jasper, but the city itself was pure gold. . . . All day the gates will never be shut" (Apoc. 21. 16 ff.). Layers of marble and gold mosaics could convey the idea of heavenly splendour. The three great arches leading into the nave were ever-open gates to the holy of holies.

The third possibility was that the small martyrium should expand into a space big enough to hold a congregation, or that the basilica should be fitted on to the martyrium. Thus about 400 the public churches over the graves of the saints in Milan were built, following the pattern developed at Antioch, as large, cruci-form martyria. In 382 St Ambrose began to build the church of the Apostles, known today as San Nazaro Maggiore. As Enrico Villa's drawing shows, it is a single-naved basilica

San Nazaro Maggiore

45 feet wide, originally with a flat ceiling; it is expanded into a cross by transepts of the same width. The transepts were each divided from the main area by an arcade of three arches, and according to Paulinus of Nola they were used for quiet meditation. The niches may have been burial-places. Similar, but corresponding more to the Latin than to the Greek cross, was the somewhat later, probably three-aisled church of San Simpliciano. The main body of the building is tightened-up by vertical divisions. San Eustorgio, San Euphemia and other martyrs' churches were of the same kind, in contrast to the simple diocesan church, the later Sant' Ambrogio. We possess an inscription for the church of the Apostles which proves that

the symbolism of the cross was very much present in the builders' minds: *Forma crucis templum est, templum victoria Christi sacra triumphalis signat imago locum* ("The church is in the form of a cross. As a symbol of triumph sanctified by Christ's victory, the cross blesses this place").

Ravenna took over the cruciform plan from Milan for the

palace church of Santa Croce with its relic of the cross. A miniature copy of this church, which has been destroyed, is provided by the chapel of St Laurence on the right-hand side of the former narthex, the so-called mausoleum of Galla Placidia. By

Santa Croce

way of Milan and other places the cruciform plan reached Gaul, where St Droctovius adopted it for St Germain-des-Prés in 556.

Various other kinds of martyrium besides the cruciform sort were copied in full-size churches. Santo Stefano in Rome followed the rotunda-plan, San Lorenzo at Milan that of the structure with four niches.

Pope Simplicius (468–83) built Santo Stefano Rotondo on the foundations of an old Roman building. An inner ring of pillars 70 feet in diameter carries the circular upper wall, which is pierced by twenty-two windows, and the tented roof.

This bright, 80-foot-high central space was originally surrounded by two low, dimly-lit outer areas. The inner of these two was undivided, but the outer one was so arranged that four open courts were roofed over and raised above the level of the parts in

Santo Stefano Rotondo

between, which were on the diagonal. The diagonal spaces were sub-divided concentrically. The inner halves served as foils, the outer ones as small atria. Thus this round building was at the same time clearly cruciform, and had a rich alternation of high and low, shallow and deep flanking spaces. It still provides one of the most impressive interiors to be found in Rome, although the outer ring has been destroyed, and since the time of Hadrian I (772-95) the centre has been supported by two big pillars.

San Lorenzo at Milan is just as unique in its own way as Stefano Rotondo. It is an artistic large martyrium, with small ones of the usual shape nestling against it, and at the same time a public church with a big atrium, a portico and the altar in the apse at the east end. The riddle of this church, made still more obscure by the rebuilding after the dome had collapsed in 1573, has still not been com-

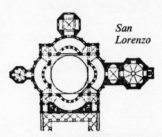

San Lorenzo

pletely solved. Scholars seemed at one time to be agreed that it was built in the sixth century and was modelled on Byzantine centralized buildings. The church of St Gregory at Etschmiadzin in Armenia, which is certainly based on Byzantine models, has a similar layout with four apses. If this dating was accepted, the difficulty arose that the subsidiary buildings, some of which certainly date from the fifth century, are right on the axis and firmly connected with the main building. Excavations have recently caused a return to the old hypothesis that San Lorenzo is a Christian Roman building, dating from the second half of the fourth century, which influenced eastern architecture. The East possessed most of the forms first, but without the Roman flair for building they would not have become the magnificent monuments that we still admire today. We must thank this flair for the existence of this huge square with a side of 75 feet, which was perhaps originally formed by four heavy pillars, and now has something of the less severe octagon about it as a result of pairs of columns set across the corners. It possesses one unique feature: the larger sides of the octagon are not broken up, as they are everywhere else, by semicircular niches; instead they allow the central space to expand into shallow hollows and attract the surrounding passages into the same rhythm.

It is only eastern architecture that displays the full range of buildings made possible by the merging of the martyrium with the basilica.

In Palestine, shrines were built at all the places where God had revealed himself in a special way: in the valley of Mamre, on Mount Tabor, Golgotha, Sion and so on. Here the most important thing was to honour Christ and his Mother. Therefore the martyria of Palestine had to be, from the start, bigger and more splendid than those elsewhere. Since they were not big enough to hold the crowds of pilgrims, basilicas were sometimes built as memorial churches or to provide extra space alongside the martyria. For example, the empress-mother built a three-aisled church of the Ascension without a transept over the grotto where, according to tradition, Christ had given his last instructions to the disciples. At Bethlehem a five-aisled basilica with solid pillars and a plain architrave

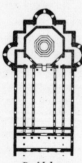
Bethlehem

was added to the octagonal shrine over the grotto where Christ was born. It is the only well-preserved example of the imperial foundations. The octagon was replaced in Justinian's time by a great apse with three bays which influenced St Maria im Kapitol and other Rhineland churches.

On the Mount of Olives there rose at the same time as the above-mentioned basilica a great rotunda of the Ascension with a wide dome and double portico. We know nothing about its interior. In the Hellenistic East, rotundas with domes resting on two-storied circles of pillars were already known at this time. The circular temple of Marnas[1] at Gaza, pulled down by the Emperor Arcadius, was a building of this kind. The same plan was chosen for the shrine over the most venerable spot in Christendom. First of all an old disgrace had to be obliterated. Two hundred years before, in order to destroy the memory of Christ's death and resurrection, the Emperor Hadrian had had

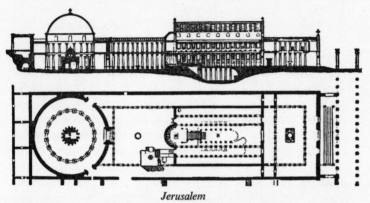

Jerusalem

the hill of Calvary and the Holy Sepulchre buried under a mass of earth, and on this platform he had erected a temple to the goddess of love. He could not guess that by doing this he was to preserve the identity of the spot through two centuries that were very dark ones for Jerusalem. The city was so often and so thoroughly destroyed, and rebuilt again on a bigger scale, that the little hill of Golgotha, like so many other holy places, would have disappeared for ever beneath 60 feet of débris. Sorrow at the desecration kept the memory of the spot alive. Constantine had it cleared. Calvary, the Holy Sepulchre and the place where the cross was discovered were enclosed within a perimeter over 450 feet long. It began in the west with a pillared courtyard which formed a small atrium. Pilgrims

[1] Palestinian deity (*Trans.*).

entered it from the street through a big gateway which, in
Eusebius' words, "by its magnificent workmanship gave all
who passed a fascinating idea of the splendour within". Three
doorways led into the first sanctuary, a five-aisled basilica with
galleries. It is the earliest known example of galleries in a
Christian church. It was reminiscent of big Hellenistic buildings
and of Jewish synagogues, which usually had galleries all
round except on the entrance side. This church could hold large
throngs of pilgrims for the night.

Eusebius praises the splendour of the gilded ceilings and
still more the *hemisphaerium*, the apse: "Round it stood twelve
pillars, in accordance with the number of the Lord's apostles,
and to crown their capitals they carried the emperor's most
precious gifts to his God, namely twelve great chased silver
mixing-bowls." Below it was the chapel of St Helena, the spot
where the cross had been discovered. On each side of the apse
was a door leading into a big inner court surrounded by colonnades. At the left-hand door the stairs up to Calvary began;
on Calvary stood a jewel-encrusted gold cross, a gift of Constantine's. Like the imperial forums at Rome, the court was
splendidly paved with marble. At its eastern end stood the
great rotunda of the Resurrection, over the burial cave.

According to a sixteenth-century drawing there were two
rings of columns round the sepulchre, one above the other, and
a row of windows between these and the dome-shaped wooden
roof. In the middle was the hewn rock containing the sepulchre.

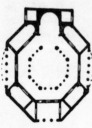
Garizim

It was enclosed and roofed in by the shrine
of the Resurrection, a circle of pillars
carrying on arcades a pierced roof of
golden beams. Between the pillars were
silver railings. In front of the entrance to
the Holy Sepulchre stood an altar, which
shows that this martyrium, like most in
the Holy Land, was intended for the celebration of the Eucharist. The divine

revelations after which martyria were named, could be
mystically repeated in the celebration of the Mass: in the
church of the Redeemer, the incarnation; in the church
dedicated to the multiplication of the loaves, the miracle of the
Eucharist; in the church of the Holy Sepulchre, the death and
resurrection of the Lord. In the valley of Josaphat a two-
storeyed rotunda was built over the grave of Mary resembling
that of the Resurrection at Jerusalem. The sanctuary of Mary
at Madaba, too, was a round building; on Mt Garizim it was
an elongated octagon. The shrines of the martyrs remained
usually small funerary chapels. Most of them stood beside the
apse. It was only seldom that they were organically linked to
the main body of the church as in the case of the chapel over the
grave of Moses on Mount Nebo. Instead they were frequently
themselves the models for bigger
churches. As early as the fourth century
an octagon was occasionally given the
four arms of a cross. A letter of St
Gregory of Nyssa allows us to reconstruct the plan of a martyr's church in
which four sides of an octagon were
expanded into the rectangular arms of
a cross, while the four diagonals were
rounded out into semicircles. As the
Apocalypse was recognized as a

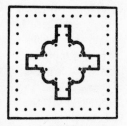

*Martyrium described by
St Gregory of Nyssa*

canonical book rather later in the East than in the West,
martyr's grave and altar were not identified so early (cf.
Apocalypse 6. 9). But the practice of putting part of a relic in
a small grave under the altar began in Palestine and Greece in
the fifth century. Thus in 415 the altar of St Demetrius at
Salonica preserved a vessel containing the saint's blood. The
church of Studios, which dated from 463, had a small crypt
in front of the apse. In Syria one of the rooms beside the
apse sometimes became a chapel for relics. Thus the body of
St Nicholas of Myra rested in the southern side-space. Big

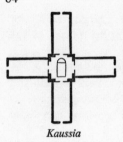

Kaussia

martyria often came into existence through the addition of new sections to an old shrine. That was the origin of the building over Jacob's well, and also of the cruciform funerary church of the martyr Babylas at Kaussia near Antioch (380). This church influenced the West by way of Milan.

The most famous example was the pilgrimage church of St John at Ephesus. According to the oldest tradition the evangelist lived on a hill near the modern township of Ajasoluk. The name keeps alive the memory of the holy theologian, the Hágios Theólogos. At the foot of the hill lay the international city of Ephesus, with its huge temple of Artemis, on the shore of a bay that has now silted up. From here John watched over the Christian communities of Asia Minor, and here he was buried. At some time after 313 a square martyrium was built over the grave. Pillars at the four corners supported a cross vault like a big baldachin. In the course of the fourth century four basilical wings were added in the form of a cross; the mauso-leum dominated

Ephesus

these four wings like a heavy tower. The eastern one had five aisles. Forty-three dioceses were subject to Ephesus. It is certain that when they built churches they thought of the patriarchal church with its central tower and sought to achieve a similar effect. A square space in front of the apse could be emphasized by pillars and its roof raised to form a bright baldachin. It is not known whether the central tower

developed in this way or in others which will be discussed later.
But it is certain that the big cruciform martyrium contributed
to the development of the basilica from a plain long nave or a
combination of nave and narrow transepts into a real cruciform
church. In the church commemorating the multiplication of the
loaves on the Sea of Galilee the transepts are no longer just
stuck-on cross-pieces, but the wide central space for the shrine
and altar. The columns of the nave are
continued along its west side. In the
lower church at Perge they continue
along the north and south walls of the
transepts, forming a dark arcade. In
the basilica of Menas at Alexandria,
founded by the Emperor Arcadius
about 400, this idea is carried to its
logical conclusion. Side-aisles and
galleries run all round the wide transepts. The apse curves out to the east
without any subsidiary branches. The

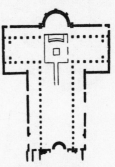

Basilica of Menas

cross, Christianity's sublimest symbol, has given the church
a wonderful unity. The altar over the martyr's grave—the
throne of the Lamb, the royal table—is no longer just the
purpose of God's house, but also its centre. The great
pilgrim churches of the early Middle Ages at Toulouse and
Compostella were to perfect the cruciform plan. The sanctuary
of Kalat Siman is similar to the church at Ephesus, but on a
still grander scale. The place lies about thirty-five miles east of
Antioch. According to Bishop Theodoret, in about 450 "a sea
of people", both Christians and pagans, streamed there from
every land from Armenia to Spain to see the living aureola,
Simeon Stylites, the martyr who lived between heaven and
earth (*aérios mártyr*). On his lofty perch, the safest refuge from
the crowd of pilgrims, he would pray with outstretched arms
through long hours of the day and night. Twice a day he
would turn to the people, preach, heal the sick and listen

Kalat Siman

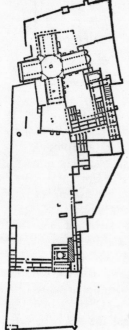

to the requests of the pilgrims. When
this life of fearful penance and glowing mysticism came to an end in 459,
the funeral ceremonies in Antioch
lasted for thirty days. Then round the
pillar a memorial church was built
which did not fall far behind that
of Jerusalem in splendour and
fame.

The ruins of Kalat Siman, the
fortress of Simeon, were discovered
and described by Vicomte de Vogüé
in 1862. The wall enclosing them was
built as a defence against the Arabs.
The visitor arrives first at a convent
with several churches and a hospice
for pilgrims. Ten minutes later he
comes to the holy fortress on its hill.
The large cluster of buildings compris-
ing the living-quarters of the priests,
a smaller church and a square

baptistery with an octagonal top is dominated by the huge pilgrimage church. Stylites' pillar was once enclosed in an octagonal space that opened north, south, east and west through big arches into four basilicas, between which were trapezium-shaped corner spaces with apses. The basilicas and the central space—the paths and the goal—were linked in the most natural way. The west–east axis was preserved, for only the eastern bas-

ilica, with its three apses, was used for the liturgy. These apses still show best today the rich and painstaking workmanship of the whole build-ing. They are framed in vigorous, finely carved arches with rosettes. The semi-circular back wall and the half-dome are made of heavy blocks of hewn stone without mortar. Out-side, against the apses, were two rows of Greek columns—one on top of the other—with an arcaded architrave. The three-storeyed

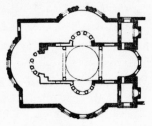

Rusafa

façade of the priest's house is still standing. It is made of long rectangular blocks and looks like the concrete skeleton of modern buildings. The whole complex is vigorously, grandly and sensibly planned. It forms a worthy memorial to the saint on the pillar, who raised himself in prayer above the earth yet remained close to human difficulties.

At Rusafa about 550 a martyrium with four apses was con-verted into a much bigger building. An inner rectangle measuring 70 feet by 33 was enlarged by the addition of a

semicircular niche to each of its sides, and connected by
columns to an outer wall of the same shape. Stairs beside the
apse led to the upper floors of the pastophoria. These solid east
towers and the raised centre made this martyrium, even without
the dome, which B. Smith would like to reconstruct, a complex
and at the same time a thoroughly unified building.

At the martyrium of the Baptist at Gerasa two small basilicas
flank the central space in accordance with the simplified plan of
Bosra.

In Lykaonia and Cappadocia, in the interior of Asia Minor,
which belonged until 450 to the Syrian province of the Church,

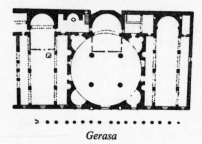

Gerasa

there are the ruins of many
small cruciform martyria.
The barrel-vaulted arms of
the cross meet in a central
tower, which is connected
by blocks placed across the
corners into an octagon;
this in turn leads into the
round of the dome. The
lengthened west side, too,
is sometimes enriched with tower-shaped erections. The apse
is built straight on to the tower without a choir. The whole
edifice consists of solid blocks of stone. These fairly small
buildings were memorial chapels, usually to the founder
of a monastery. The cruciform plan was adopted later in
Cappadocia for parish churches. It was here that it gained
its clear, mathematical form: the intersection was picked out,
and the spot where the nave and transepts crossed was
emphasized. This crown of the whole building, illuminated
from above and pointing upwards, also became its unit of
measure. Already the building is articulated inside and outside
by cross-arches. The gradation of the sections is strongly
emphasized. Outside this region the cruciform church is rare. A
Syrian example is the church of Elias in the Hauruan, which

dates from 532. It has a flat stone ceiling, a square choir and a dome over the intersection. The square choir is one of the most important innovations that the cruciform church brought to the West on its journey through the lands that border the Aegean and the Adriatic. It had appeared in the East since the Byzantine domed basilica had introduced a space between the centralized dome and the apse.

Western pilgrims took many fresh ideas home with them from Syria, especially from the shrine of Simeon. Just as in the early stages of its development the single-aisled cruciform martyrium had been used as a model for the church of the Apostles at Milan, so now the three-aisled cruciform basilica was imitated at Salona (Spalato). It is Kalat Siman with a rectangular intersection marked off by arcades, and so not a unitary building.

THE PICTURES THAT ADORNED MARTYRIA

Immediately over the grave, perhaps in an apse, the martyr was frequently portrayed in the attitude of an Orante: in death the blood witness has come to resemble the crucified Christ. He has completed Christ's sufferings in his own body. There can be no doubt about this relationship, for in old pictures of the crucifixion, such as that on the door of Santa Sabina, Christ stands as an Orante in front of the cross, which meant nothing to pagans. The dome shows the Lamb on the mountain of paradise, or the Father's hand with the wreath. Often Christ hands the crown to the martyr, or those who have testified with their blood bring their crowns to Christ, because he is the martyr's strength and triumphs in them. The forms are borrowed from the imperial world. Christ is the heavenly sovereign in a golden palace, his saints are high dignitaries, victorious warriors. Basilius suggests that Christ should be portrayed as the Agōnothétēs, the organizer of the great contest, the martyrs as victorious competitors and the howling demons as defeated opponents.

Gregory of Nyssa describes the pictures in the martyrium of St Theodore at Euchaita: the great deeds of Christ the athlete, his resistance, his sufferings, the cruelty of the tyrant, and his glorious death. The martyrdom of St Euphemia was fully portrayed in her martyrium at Chalcedon.

But soon conceptions divide. The western Church sees the membership of Christ in the martyr already accomplished on earth and therefore portrays him right down the centuries—often very realistically—in his suffering and death. After Chrysostom, Byzantine art sees the martyr in a different light: only in the splendour of heaven is he completely incorporated in Christ. His glorified body possesses a life compared with which earthly life is little more than death. To portray the saints in their earthly guise would therefore be tantamount to diminishing their eternal glory. So they are shown in a golden light, a solemn beauty, an unreal attitude which seemed to the naturalistic nineteenth century like lifeless rigidity, but is now regarded again as one of the first attempts to represent the supernatural world.

CHAPTER IV

THE EARLY CHURCH'S IMAGE OF CHRIST

According to Joh. Kollwitz, the theme of the oldest Christian art was man praying to the God who saved him. The Old Testament provided almost more stimulus than the New. In New Testament pictures the work of the Redeemer was more important than his person. To start with, there was no ideal conception of Christ, but the symbol of the fisher of men, of the shepherd and teacher, as described in the Scriptures and ancient wisdom.

The language of symbols removed the supernatural content of the revelation from the realm of the all-too-near and comprehensible, where it might have been misunderstood, and made the search no easier for the initiated. Abercius uses these veiled terms in his inscription: "Everywhere faith drew me on, and put before me as food in every place a fish from the spring, exceptionally big and pure, which a pure maiden had caught. This he always gave to his friends as a meal, pouring out sweet wine, offering wine mixed with water and bread."

In the second and third centuries the features of the spiritual Christ were too different for a universal type to come into being. The Docetists and Gnostics took the view that Christ seemed different to everyone, the image varying according to each individual's power of comprehension and personal worth. The *Shepherd of Hermas*, a late-second-century book, speaks of the extra-dimensional form of the "great son of God". The

91

Carpocratians attempted quite early on to draw a historical portrait of Christ. Their efforts were summarily rejected because they were furthest of all from understanding the secret of God-made-man. The orthodox, too, held opinions that differed a good deal. Scholars like Justin, Tertullian, Clement of Alexandria and St Hippolytus believed, in accordance with Isaias 53, that Christ's divinity had purposely hidden itself in an inconspicuous body. The pagan Celsus used this as an argument against the divinity of Christ which did not fail to make its impression: if Christ was God, he said, he would have been bound to excel all men in beauty, for beauty is an essential characteristic of the divine. For the ancient world, beauty and goodness were inseparably linked in the concept of *kalokagathia*. So towards 300 belief in the heavenly Lord who would return in glory led to a portrait that corresponded equally to the spiritual image of popular literature, the learned logos-theology and the ancient conception of the gods. It consisted of a youthful, handsome, idealized human figure symbolizing the immortal divine nature. Sarcophagi allow us to see clearly the origin and development of this image of Christ. At the beginning of the fourth century the Saviour of the poor, the philosopher-Christ, is still recalled by the costume: pallium, sandals and pilgrim's staff, which is now becoming the emblem of the miracle-worker. However, the intention is no longer to show the humility of Christ's assumption of humanity, but the glory of the only-begotten son of the Father. On sarcophagi round about 300 we find a timeless, youthful, manly Christ modelled on youthful heroes (see illustration 17). In the early days after the Edict of Toleration, the genii in the pictures of the seasons normally found on triumphal arches are young sons of the gods, superior to the flux of time, promising the empire good fortune and lasting duration and forming the model for a somewhat more tender type of Christ. From these prototypes Christian art creates, in the so-called "beautiful" style of the middle of the century, the picture of the youthfully innocent son of God with which we are familiar from sarcophagi, ivory carvings and the famous statuette in the Lateran Museum (see cover picture).

We find this lovable, pure picture of Christ particularly in the miracle scenes intended to show God's love for humanity. Because what it could express was limited, we find it supplemented by another, still more closely related to the ancient conception of the ruler. Rulers loved to identify themselves with Zeus, the lord and saviour of the world. Distantly based on such pictures, and continuing the conception of Christ as the teacher, arose the type of the bearded Christ. This can express the wisdom of the lawgiver, the majesty of the universal judge and the sublimity of the omnipotent ruler better than the youthful Christ. Both types reflect the new attitude to emperor and empire.

In accordance with Scripture, the primitive Church had accepted the State as the guarantor of order and interceded on its behalf in its prayers. It had resisted the State when it had put itself in God's place and usurped functions outside its domain. The martyr Polycarp opposed to the earthly Caesar his own King, Christ, whose realm is not of this world. In the third century St Hippolytus described the Roman empire as a satanic opponent of Christ's kingdom. The primitive Church was a Church of martyrs because Christianity and emperor-worship were irreconcilable opponents. But in the fourth century there had been an unparalleled spiritual revolution, and it was a question of putting the idea of a Christian empire on a firm foundation.

Constantine recognized that the Christian religion was a powerful spiritual force and, as a politician, came to terms with it. He gave it freedom in order, through it, to assure the internal peace of the empire. The

Church became an imperial Church, its law became the law of
the State, its bishops were put on the same footing as the highest
dignitaries of the State. The bishop of Rome received, with the
emperor, the right to the genuflection, the kissing of the foot
and the ring. In the West the popes fought a hard fight against
the confusion of the spiritual and the secular spheres and
suffered much persecution as a result. As for the East, which
in the following centuries was more powerful in almost every
respect, the court of Bishop Eusebius laid the foundations of
a close—in fact, too close—relationship between Church and
State. He says in his speech of praise on the thirtieth anniversary of Constantine's accession: "Christ, the word of God, is
Lord of the world. But through him our emperor, beloved of
God, rules all earthly things as the image of the heavenly emperor." He yields a great deal to Christ, only to win it back in
the grace of God as Holy Emperor and Pontifex Maximus,
lord over State and Church, with greater dignity than he ever
enjoyed before. Title, throne, purple robe, halo, enthronement
on the vault of heaven or the globe of earth, the stance on the
clouds or the defeated dragon, the ruler's gesture of the
raised hand, the acclamation and presentation of gifts by
dignitaries, the reception of the gifts on veiled hands, the
obliquely set throne-room, the baldachin as a miniature copy of
heaven, the names aula and sacrarium (= palace and throne-
room, literally "sanctuary") for church and altar-space, the
orientation of the building usual in sun-worship, incense,
candles, genuflection: all these things and many others pass
over, partly in the fourth century, completely in the sixth, from
the emperor to Christ the Lord. Saints receive the badges of
rank of high officials, the apostles the emperor's purple toga
and Our Lady the costume of the empress.

The rich pictorial decorations of the early basilicas have
almost completely vanished. They have been partly preserved,
in often cursory copies, in the funerary art of the sarcophagi
and catacombs. The development of the conception of Christ in

the fourth century is shown most clearly on sarcophagi. Now that the Church is at peace, people are no longer content with a symbol that merely hints; they want a clear narration of the events described in the Bible. In the fourth century sixty new themes are added to the less than twenty of the third century. From the Old Testament, for example, we meet the creation of Adam and Eve, Pharaoh's destruction in the Red Sea, the misfortunes of Job, the ascension of Elias, and the slaughter of the dragon by Daniel. From the New Testament we find the Christmas story, the Sermon on the Mount, several of the miracles, scenes from the Passion, the handing of the keys to Peter and the Ascension. In addition to these, there are four scenes from the Acts of the Apostles and eight from the apocryphal legends about St Peter.

The great themes of the fourth century are Christ's miracles and acts of kindness as a revelation of his glory, Christ's struggle and victory in his own Passion and in that of his disciples, Christ's foundation of his kingdom and his dominion.

Constantine's age loved miracle-workers. Over against the ever-repeated picture of the raising of Lazarus, we find Peter's miraculous production of water, by which he is supposed to have converted Roman legionaries.

Master and disciple, the founder of the Church and his first representative, confront each other as benefactors. Sometimes they are related to the Orante in the middle representing the Church. Like the baptism of Christ in the third century, this water from the rock is now the symbol of the water of life, the beginning of a new life, just as the raising of the dead is the guarantee of eternal life.

Frequently the sacrifice of Isaac is added as a prototype of the sacrifice of Christ; it deepens the meaning of the miracle scenes: the awakener of the dead has by his own death procured life. With admirable restraint art begins to show Christ's human feelings, when he bends towards the sisters at the raising of Lazarus. Big cycles of pictures, without any strict arrangement, but full of atmosphere and harmony, appear on sarcophagi with friezes. The healing of the blind man and of the woman with an issue of blood, the multiplication of the loaves and the miracle at Cana are often grouped round the prophecy of Peter's denial or the Church escorted by Peter and Paul.

The very numerous pictures of Peter in the fourth century, many of which portray him as a shepherd with a lamb on his shoulder, do not testify to the primacy of St Peter in the strict dogmatic sense, for very frequently Paul is shown as well on the same scale and with equal dignity (see illustration 5). But his special position is clearly enough expressed. Some fifty times sarcophagi show the prophecy of the denial and the handing over of the keys. These signify the close linking of the apostle to Christ by the pardoning of his fault and the eminence of his office.

About the middle of the century Christus-Basileus (Christ the King) becomes the great theme. The basilica receives the significance implied in its name. An anti-Arian formula of this time—Christ, God of Gods, King of Kings, Lord of Lords—takes visible shape. *Christ the Lawgiver* is an early form of the ruler-idea in late Constantinian times. In a side-niche in S. Costanza, which was probably designed in connection with the mosaic of St Peter in the apse, Christ puts the scroll containing the law into Peter's veiled hands to the applause of Paul. He still has the hair-style and beard of the philosopher, but the costume, halo and gesture of the emperor. The scene resembles the audience given by the departing emperor to a high official, to whom he entrusts full powers. "The apostles are indeed officials, to whom the whole world is entrusted", says John Chrysostom. Lambs, palms and the holy cities of Jerusalem and Bethlehem symbolize the apocalyptic sphere.

On pillar- and tree-sarcophagi the struggle and victory of Christ are portrayed. Much is borrowed from imperial symbolism. Since in the more and more dangerous struggle of the previous century against the emperor's enemies the continued

1. Christ as sun-god. Mosaic in a mausoleum under St Peter's. End of the third century.

2. Cubiculum in the catacomb of St Peter and St Marcellinus. Fourth century.

3. *Coemeterium Iordanorum, with paintings of the third and fourth century.*

4. *Meal of the blessed. Peace and Love serve the guests. Catacomb of St Peter and St Marcellinus. Fourth century.*

5. *Peter and Paul. Gold leaf drawing on base of glass bowl. Fourth century.*

6. *Susanna as a lamb between wolves. Praetexta Catacomb. Third century.*

MVNIFICENTIA LEONIS XIII. P. M.

7. *Sarcophagus from the Via Salaria. Third century. Shepherd and Orante (or Orans) between the dead husband and wife.*

8. *Three pictures of Christ from the poly-chrome fragments of the Thermae Museum. c. 300.*

9. *The praetorium of Musmieh in Syria. Second century.*

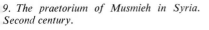

10. *Sarcophagus from Santa Maria Antiqua. End of third century.*

11. Passion-sarcophagus in the Lateran Museum. c. 340.

12. Christ carrying the cross. Ivory panel in London, 425,

13. Altar rails of San Clemente. Fourth and thirteenth centuries

14. *Christ between Peter and Paul. Centrepiece of the sarcophagus of Junius Bassus. 359.*

15. *Santa Sabina. 422–32.*

16. *Handle of a bronze lamp. Fourth century. Campo Santo Museum.*

17. *Raising of Lazarus. Sarcophagus in the Thermae Museum. Fourth century.*

18. *Crucifixion on the wooden door of Santa Sabina. 422–32.*

19. *Christ and the apostles. Domitilla catacomb. Fourth century.*

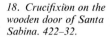

20. Mosaic in the apse of S. Pudenziana at Rome. c. *400.*

21. Christ, in SS. Cosma e Damiano.
c. *530.*

22. Christ and the Church. A scene on the wooden door of Santa Sabina. 422–32.

23. *San Apollinare in Classe, Ravenna. 535–49.*

24. *The Empress Theodora; apse of San Vitale. 538–47.*

25. *Christ the Emperor. Archiepiscopal chapel. After 500.*

26. *San Vitale, Ravenna. 538–47.*

27. *Hagia Sophia, Constantinople. 532–7. Drawing by Fossati.*

28. *Apse of church of Dêr Termanin in Syria. c. 500.*

29. *Birth of Christ. Adoration of the Magi. Ivory. Sixth century.*

30. *Madonna in S. Maria Nuova, Rome. Seventh–eighth centuries.*

31. *Madonna in the crypt of San Clemente, Rome. Eighth century.*

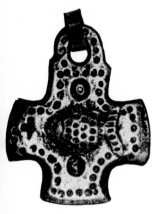

32. Cross with fish. Southern France; period of the migrations.

33. Crucifix from S. Maria Antiqua, Rome. Eighth century.

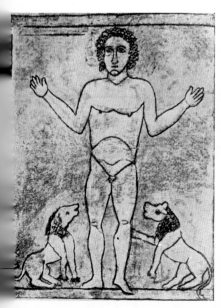

34. Daniel between the lions. Gaul. Fifth–sixth centuries.

35. Gravestone from Niederdollendorf. End of seventh century.

36. *Christ as victor on a white horse (Apoc. 19. 11). Coptic relief, sixth century.*

37. *Altar of Count Ratschis in San Martino at Cividale. Front. Eighth century.*

38. *Right-hand side: Adoration of the Magi.*

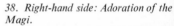

39. *Book - cover from Genoels- Elderen, End of eighth century,* →

40. Tassilo chalice at Kremsmünster.
775–81.

41. Stele from Moselkern.
End of seventh century.

42. St Michael's, Fulda.
822.

43. Initial letter from the
Folchart Psalter at St
Gallen. Ninth century.

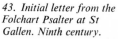

44. *Mosaic in the apse of Santa Maria in Domnica, Rome. Ninth century.*

45. *Ivory panel of the diptych at Rambona.*
c. 900.

46. *Crowning of the virtues. Manuscript at*
St Gallen. Late ninth century.

47. *Christ: cover of the Codex Aureus. After 870.*

existence of the Roman empire had only been assured by outstanding emperors like Aurelian, Diocletian and Constantine—great generals and great statesmen as well—the word imperator had come to be associated with military service under famous standards, with struggle and victory, triumph and coronation. Just as earlier the hand of God crowned the emperor, so now the Father's hand gives the laurel wreath to Christ. Just as the emperor presented the wreath of victory to his generals, so Christ rewards the disciples, the *collegae crucis Christi* as Prudentius calls them, who are helped on to victory by his own triumph. Like subsidiary leaders, they stand round the emperor Christ as *amici*, trusted friends, who have free access to him at all times. The finest example of this sort of scene is the sarcophagus of Junius Bassus, prefect of the city of Rome. It dates from 359, and is in the crypt of St Peter's. In the middle of the lower scene Christ, identified as imperator by the imperial eagle of victory, rides between Adam and Eve and Daniel to the sacrificial death. The corners show the suffering Job and Paul on the way to martyrdom; by his death, the soldier of Christ wins a share in Christ's glory.

In the left-hand section of the upper scene are portrayed the sacrifice of Isaac and the arrest of Peter, in the right-hand section Christ's own struggle: his appearance before Pilate and the latter washing his hands. The middle of the upper scene shows the heavenly sphere of the victor. Christ is enthroned between the princes of the apostles, he is shown as the blessed son of God, eternally youthful, radiant and mild, in the act of giving a blessing, holding the roll containing the Gospels, with his feet resting on the billowing cloak of the ancient sky-god (see illustration 14).

How these pictures of struggle and victory give rise to richer and richer passion-cycles is described in another chapter. The conception of Christ the King transforms old pictures and produces new ones. The homely shepherd of the catacombs develops into the royal shepherd in the mausoleum of Galla

Placidia. In the archi-episcopal chapel at Ravenna, Christ stands, like Constantine at the door of his palace in earlier pictures, in the uniform of a general on the bodies of vanquished monsters. In the last third of the century the picture of the lawgiver and imperator broadens into that of the cosmocrator, the ruler of the world. The visions in the Apocalypse of the city of God and the throne of the universal ruler, which the seer compared with the luxury of the kings of Pergamum and the Roman emperors, become a rich source of new pictures. The court ceremonial of the now Christian emperor provides many details for the pictures of heavenly splendour. On the triumphal arch we find in the middle the throne of the Lamb or the Lamb himself in the midst of the seven lamps, the four creatures and the twenty-four elders, who bring their crowns on veiled hands. Behind is the city of God, the heavenly Jerusalem in the guise of the earthly one; for example in the magnificent mosaic in the apse of St. Pudenziana (see illustration 20). The mighty enthroned Christ, called by the title of his book *conservator ecclesiae S. Pudentianae*—protector of the church—to whom the two women are bringing golden wreaths, is reminiscent of old pictures of Jupiter Conservator. Golden garlands were presented to the emperor by the high dignitaries and governors of the provinces. The subject peoples brought gold as a gift of honour. The triumphal arch of St Paul, the best preserved one, bears a huge portrait of the head and shoulders of Christ with a halo and the twenty-four elders. Earlier on, the emperor was portrayed in this way on the triumphal arch of some basilicas. There are hints of courtly prototypes in the retinue of the little king in the childhood pictures in Santa Maria Maggiore and in the train of the royal mother in the cathedral of Parenzo. The gilded throne with a golden crown represented the emperor. The throne with the Gospels on wall-mosaics, or the real throne with the Scriptures in the middle of the councils of the fourth and fifth centuries, indicated the presence of Christ.

The so-called city-gate sarcophagi, too, of the time of Theodosianus (380–410), announce the majesty of the Lord. A usually bearded Christ stands or sits, serious and sublime, as the universal ruler in the twelve-gated heavenly city, round him the senate of the apostles, who will judge the twelve tribes of Israel.

The liturgy, as well as art, draws on the Apocalypse, and it, too, borrows elements from imperial protocol. The solemn silence customary at the entrance of the emperor now greets the appearance of Christ on the altar. The solemn announcement of the Gospel with candles and incense resembles the proclamation of an imperial law. Many acclamations, that is, cries of supplication or homage, passed over from the imperial service to the Christian liturgy: "Kyrie eleison", "dignus et justus", "gloria et laus".

Many imperial titles were borrowed, too, such as *Salvator* = rescuer, saviour of the world, *Largitor* = generous ruler, *Pius et clemens* = mild to subjects and defeated opponents. It was usually felt appropriate to borrow the unofficial names; similarly, in the visual arts, parallels that were too obvious, such as the jagged crown in the picture of Christ as the sun, were generally avoided.

THE FESTIVAL OF CHRISTMAS

The christianization of the worship of the sun-god produced the Christmas festival. For the first three centuries of the Christian era the arrival of the divine child and the summons from darkness into light were celebrated at the Epiphany; the festival was symbolized by the adoration of the Magi. It was precisely the idea of Christ as the light of the world that gradually led to the development of the Christmas festival. As early as 200, that is, before the connection with the worship of the Roman emperors as the sun, the comparison of Christ with the sun was becoming quite frequent in Christian writers: what the sun is in the universe, Christ is in the realm of salvation. That is why people prayed facing the east. When Scripture calls Christ "sun of righteousness, sun of salvation", Clement of Alexandria has no scruples about taking over the imagery of pagan mythology and calling him as well the "Helios (sun-god) that traverses the universe". In a pre-Constantinian mausoleum under St Peter's a damaged mosaic of Christ as the sun-god has been preserved (see illustration 1). Although small in size, it is impressive in design. Christ is all light, with a fiery glance that is full of life. The picture of the ruler with the twelve spikes of light, symbols of the stars, which had been developed in late Hellenistic times and had long before crystallized into a schematic design, here assumes a higher significance. It gains a victorious, glowing life and shows how organic the link between antiquity and Christianity could be, even in the domain of emperor-worship, once mortally dangerous for Christians. In the course of the third century the emperors, especially the Syrian ones, allowed themselves to be venerated more and more expressly as sun-god. Aurelian (270–5) made December 25th, the sun-god's birthday, an imperial festival. After the victory of the Church it was taken over as the birthday of the true sun, as Christmas.

Verbum coro opportuno tempore
Conditor solis, conditus sub sole.

("The word was made flesh at a fitting time: the sun's creator came into the world on the sun's birthday.")

(Augustine, *Sermon* 187.)

So the depiction of Christmas scenes begins in the fourth century. The word has been made flesh, says one of the oldest of such scenes—a faded fresco under San Sebastiano—with striking clarity. Above are the head and shoulders of the son of God in the radiance of the sun's disk, below the tiny form of God incarnate in the crib, flesh that can suffer and will die. A relief of 343 also shows this renunciation: the child, without Mary and Joseph, between animals and shepherds. Ancient

pictures of the discovery of Romulus
and Remus by shepherds may have
served as a model. But usually the
mother, her strength unimpaired, sits
proudly under a sheltering roof by the
side of the crib (see illustration 29).
Eastern art, on the other hand, early emphasizes the "born of woman" by
depicting Mary in a lying or half-lying
position. The souvenirs of pilgrims at
Monza suggest that the mosaic in the
grotto at Bethlehem was the prototype
of these pictures. This would explain the

cave as well. Joseph is usually absent from the oldest pictures because Christ is removed from the purely human sphere and
must be shown as the son of the eternal Father. After the
Council of Ephesus (431) not only Mary's motherhood, but
also Joseph's position of honour as head of the family, is more
strongly emphasized. He appears as the Virgin Mother's husband and sits with her opposite the child. The most beautiful
expression of the marriage bond between Mary and Joseph is
an ivory carving on the cathedra of Maximian at Ravenna

(546–56); in the upper half the angel
speaks to Joseph in the dream, below an angel escorts the couple to
Bethlehem. Mary is sitting on the
donkey and has laid her arm round
Joseph's shoulder for help and encouragement. He supports her carefully with his right hand. In the
Christmas scene on the bishop's

throne he watches over the child, while in the foreground Mary
lies on a pillow and listens to the complaint of one of the midwives about her withered hand. She doubted the virgin birth
and is healed by the touch of the child. The influence of the

so-called apocryphal gospels is evident: only too evident on another picture in which Joseph reproaches Mary with her pregnancy and makes her drink poisoned water as an ordeal to prove her innocence. Since the four gospels said so little about the birth and childhood of Jesus, from the second century onwards imaginative legends full of wonders grew up; their pious object was to supply the missing details, but they often displayed little insight or taste. They were collected in the so-called proto-gospel of St James. It tells the story of Joachim and Anna and describes the birth of Mary, her visit to the temple, her betrothal to the eighty-nine-year-old Joseph, whose staff had blossomed of its own accord, Joseph's doubts of her innocence and his enlightenment by the angel. After that follows the detailed story of Christmas, with the tale of the believing and unbelieving midwives, up to the adoration of the Magi. An improved fifth-century Latin version of these stories, which went by the name of the gospel of the pseudo-Matthew, found its way to the West and provided artists for a thousand years with the themes for innumerable devotional pictures. Even Dürer's "Life of Mary" cannot be understood without reference to these apocryphal stories. In the East these stories soon gave rise to the great cycles of pictures which are recorded in the painter's book of Mt Athos and which provided the West, too, with a good deal of artistic stimulus. Byzantine art sometimes took over from the West the early type of sitting Virgin Mary for the Christmas scene, but much more frequently, indeed almost always, we meet in western pictures until the Gothic period the Byzantine conception, with Mary lying down and turning tenderly to the child or reverently remaining at a distance from him.

CHAPTER V

THE LOGOS ON THE CROSS

Pictures of the Passion and the crucifixion did not begin late because Christians had to be gradually educated to regard the symbol of shame as the symbol of victory. As early as the second century pagans accused Christians of praying to a cross. Minucius Felix explained that this veneration was meant for Christ himself. The cross was discerned in every natural phenomenon: in the ploughshare, in the anchor, in the mast of a ship crossed at right-angles by the yard, in the dolphin transfixed by the trident, in the flying bird. St Hippolytus says that Christ on the cross spreads his arms over the faithful like the protecting wings of an eagle. By 200, according to Tertullian, the frequent use of the sign of the cross was already an old-established custom: "At every moment, on entering or leaving a house, when we dress or do up our shoes, when we wash, eat, light a lamp, go to bed or sit down, whenever we meet together, we make the sign of the cross on our foreheads" (*De coron. mil.* c. 3). The primitive Church lived in the expectation of the end of the world. The second coming of Christ and the cross as symbol of the Son of man belonged inseparably together. People thought of him when they prayed facing the east with outstretched arms. On the other hand, the primitive Church did not locate the redemptive work of Christ so exclusively as we do in the Passion, but rather in his earthly life as a whole, in his teaching, his miracles and the sacraments he instituted. "Through the incarnation man is given back his lost

103

likeness to God and is thus redeemed," says Irenaeus (*Adversus Haereses*, III, 19, 1). In the hard days of persecution, by the graves of the dead, the fact of salvation and Christ's giving of his life were more important than the details of the Passion. In the figure of the shepherd both were expressed: "I give my life for my sheep" and "No one shall tear them away from my hand." The cross in the form we know appears some twenty times in the catacombs, much more frequently as anchor and trident, the Greek letter tau, and the Orans or Orante with arms outstretched like a cross. Fear of profanation of the holiest may have contributed to this result, but there is another still more important reason. In spite of the decline of classical ideals, the art of the third and fourth centuries is still a relatively naturalistic art. This very fact was bound to deter artists from depicting the crucifixion. The sublime idea of redemption could not be made into the act of execution with which fourth-century Christians were still familiar from their own experience. The paradox of the death of immortal God either forbade any attempt at portrayal or else necessitated more symbolism than art had hitherto employed.

Before the depiction of the crucifixion, veneration of the cross reached a high point in the fourth century. It began when Constantine made the cross the public emblem of victory, and put it in the hand of the statue of himself erected by the citizens of Rome. It grew through reports of the appearance of the cross and above all through the discovery of the "true cross of Christ" at Jerusalem. Crowds of pilgrims flocked there, and parts of the holy cross reached the West.

On Golgotha stood a jewel-encrusted cross. As early as the fourth century the cross was linked with the mysterious tree of life in paradise. The jewelled cross in the Pontian catacomb is putting out shoots. The jewelled cross on the hill of paradise with the four rivers is always intended to represent the tree of life; so is Christ himself on the hill of paradise, as frequent comparisons in literature show.

The first real passion sarcophagus (No. 171 in the Lateran Museum) dates from about 340; it is of considerable significance in the history of piety (see illustration 11). The victory of Christianity caused such joy that the Passion was portrayed not as the humiliation of God incarnate but as the glorification of the son of God. The symbolism of emperor-worship was taken over for this purpose. In the central scene, the eagle, the imperial emblem, carries down from heaven—sun and moon are depicted over the wide arch of the sky—the imperial laurel wreath with Christ's name in it above the "undefeated cross". It is the labarum, Constantine's standard in the fight against Maxentius. Here it is returned to the Imperator Christ as his own standard. The two watchers at the grave are like sentries posted to guard the standard. The next scene to the left shows not the crowning with thorns, but the crowning of an emperor. So here a legionary sets the jewelled wreath on the head of a youthful, majestic Christ. On the extreme left, Simon of Cyrene carries the cross at the command of the soldier in the service of Christ the King. On the right, Christ confesses his kingship to Pilate, whose struggle with his own conscience is clearly portrayed. By suffering Christ enters into his glory. The end-pictures on sarcophagus No. 174, the sacrifice of Isaac and the trial before Pilate, show that through the Passion Christ wins his empire. In the middle he is enthroned as heavenly ruler on the outspread cloak of the ancient sky-god, and gives the law to Peter. In just the same way, as Fr Gerke has pointed out, on the arch of Galerius at Salonica, the two senior emperors Diocletian and Maxentius sit over a sky-god, while the junior emperors Galerius and Constantine stand beside them. Peter receives the scroll with veiled hands. An ivory casket from the third quarter of the century, the Lipsanothek in Brescia, shows five scenes from the Passion in the same style: Gethsemane, depicted not as a mental struggle but as a calm, straightforward acceptance of the sacrifice, the arrest, Peter's denial, the trial before the high priests and the appearance before Pilate.

Still more significant are four ivory carvings in the British Museum, originally the sides of a casket dating from about 425. One shows, in a vigorous, diagonally composed scene, Christ carrying the cross between Pilate washing his hands and Peter's denial. Between the moral cowardice of his opponents and the weakness of his friends he carries the cross like a standard (see illustration 12). The second tablet shows for the first time the unveiled picture of Christ crucified. Christ stands —the feet are not nailed—like an emperor, with outstretched arms and raised head, in front of a triumphal cross; he is identified by the inscription as king of the Jews, and by the halo as the exalted son of God. Mary and John stand side by side. On the other side Longinus gives the fatal thrust. It is the death of consummation. On the left Judas dies the death of despair. Thus the cross is the judge's throne and the entrance to glory. The third tablet shows the women and guards at the grave, and the fourth the transfigured Christ with Thomas and two other apostles.

Equally well known is the somewhat later picture of the crucifixion on the wooden door of Santa Sabina on the Aventine, the centre-piece of seven small scenes from the Passion (see illustration 18). Christ, depicted as a vigorous bearded man, distinguished from the thieves by his size, stands in the attitude of an Orante in front of city buildings. It is an early, powerful expression of the phrase in the creed: *crucifixus pro nobis*. Christ is nailed between two malefactors and at the same time raised above them as "the great son of God". The larger-than-life figure of Christ as the symbol of the divine nature, alluded

Gem

to as early as the second century by the "Shepherd of Hermas", could be seen by the carver of Santa Sabina on earlier, probably Gnostic, gems. He, too, closes his cycle with the return of Christ at Easter and the ascension.

Part of one of St Leo's Easter sermons seems to have been suggested by pictures such as these: the Lord transformed the cross that he carried into the sceptre of his might. To the godless, it seemed shameful; to believers, a great mystery was revealed: the glorious victor over the devil, the powerful warrior against the hostile powers carried like a king the trophy of his victory (*Sermon* 59, 4).

The crucifixion pictures of the London ivory and the door of Santa Sabina cannot be the oldest, for the theme would not have been essayed in this bold form for the first time on the door of a church. The inspiration must have come from Syria and Palestine. For pilgrims to Jerusalem the reminder of the Lord's sufferings was the most impressive part of their experience. Little souvenirs in the form of crosses, medallions, phials of water from the Jordan, oil from the lamps in the church of the Holy Sepulchre and earth from the Holy Land were intended to keep the experience alive. About 350 Makrina, the saintly sister of Gregory of Nyssa, wore a small cross as a phylactery, that is, a protection, as preachers advised, in order to drive out the earlier amulets. "The cross is the mark of the believer and the terror of demons", says Cyril of Jerusalem. To the plain cross was added a half-length portrait of Christ, and there were sketches of the two thieves, Adam and Eve and Mary and John, as shown by the later Monza phials, which are based on early prototypes in Palestine. Soon there were attempts to give the whole figure of Christ in relief, or to incise it, in order to increase the efficacy of the emblem. A certain shyness made these pictures so small that they could only be used for private devotion. Beyond the universal human desire to give things a visible form, Syrian and Palestinian realism was probably the most important factor

Phial from Monza

in the production of these little pictures. It was not superficial realism, but that of an inner vision.

The intellectual divisions of the fifth-century Christological disputes are clearly reflected in pictures of the cross. The Monophysites, who believed that Christ had only one, divine nature and regarded his human nature as mere appearance, rejected all pictures of the crucifixion, in order to preserve the son of God from any suspicion of human weakness. Their jewelled crosses without the body of Christ influenced the West by way of Ravenna, for many of the Byzantine emperors were favourably disposed towards them. The crucifixion is absent from the great Passion cycle of San Apollinare Nuovo. About 600 a picture of the crucified Christ clad only in a loin-cloth aroused attention and opposition in Gaul. It was only the Council in Trullo at Constantinople in 692 that prescribed the copying of the figure of Christ on the cross instead of the Lamb. The Nestorians, the opponents of the Monophysites, took Christ's human nature seriously, but denied its essential connection with the divine nature. They were condemned at Ephesus in 431, but their crucifixes, which the sources soon mention, could be taken over by the Church in the struggle against the Monophysites. The depiction of Christ crucified was regarded as visible acceptance of the dogma of the real incarnation and Passion of Christ. At the same time the Nestorian error had to be avoided. Even in death, Christ had to appear as the Lord of life, otherwise the early Church regarded the picture as blasphemous.

At Constantinople, where this difficulty was appreciated particularly clearly, a picture of the crucifixion intended as a model was set up quite early in Justinian's church of the Apostles. Two ancient descriptions, which seem to contradict each other in important points, are in reality complementary, and enable us to see the deep meaning of the picture. According to Nicholas Mesarites, Christ hung on the cross in a sleeveless colobium *dying*, "clad in dark raiment, the sign of suffering and burial, his hands spread out wide and thus embracing all the peoples of the earth". According to Kostantinos Rhodios, he hung on the wood of the cross between the malefactors, between the spear and sponge-bearers, between Mary and John, with his side pierced, *dead*. One description concentrates on the open eyes, the other on the pierced side. The figure was that of a dead man, who is at the same time alive. The following pictures also pose this riddle. The Syrian miniature in the Rabulas codex of 586 tells the story of the crucifixion in decidedly realistic terms, with mourning women, soldiers dicing, spear and sponge-bearers and the two thieves. But all this serves a symbolism that is just as decided. As well as the historical facts, the idea of the redemption is given concrete form. Christ stands over the earth in the colobium, the high priest who offers a sacrifice and gives a blessing. The thieves, too, are made relatively big, because they reflect the power of the crucified Christ. Both are believers, but the left-hand one no longer has the strength to hope. Spear and sponge-bearers proclaim that the Scriptures, God's eternal plan of salvation, have been fulfilled. Christ's side is pierced, while the countenance is fully awake. The same characteristics occur in the crucifixion on a casket of somewhat later date in the Sancta Sanctorum chapel. It is designed on the same plan, but simplified and clarified by strict symmetry, which puts John with the gospel on the left of Christ, as always from now onward. This picture leads on to the well-known eighth-century fresco in Santa Maria Antiqua in the Forum at Rome (see illustration 33). All that the early Church demanded of a crucifixion is fulfilled in this Byzantine work. The victim is at the same time God enthroned. The historical fact is at the same time the mystery which is at work in the present. Mary is the image of the Church, the second Eve, all courage and readiness, John is the inspired witness and evangelist. Longinus and Stephaton are smaller in proportions but important to the composition and significant in their function. The blood gushes from the wound in Christ's side. In

Irish crucifix

spite of the lance-thrust, which according to Scripture is the sure sign of his death, Christ's eyes are wide open and full of life. The usual explanation is that pictures such as this compress several phases in the train of events, in order to make the meaning more concise. But here the phases are too contradictory: obvious death and obvious life in the same figure. By adducing copious examples Alois Grillmeier has made a deeper meaning probable, which is also confirmed in the case of later pictures by inscriptions. According to the ancient conception, with which both pagans and Jews were familiar, the open, unsleeping eye was the symbol of the immortal, ever-watchful Godhead: "Such a guardian has Israel, one who is never weary, never sleeps" (Ps. 120. 4). "Our Lord slept a little in the body on the cross, but as God he kept the eyes of the Godhead open", says St Eulogius of Alexandria. In these pictures the dogma of the indissoluble union of the two natures in Christ is given concrete expression. It is "the logos on the cross".

The crucifix reached the Franks direct from the south or by by way of Ireland, England and Scotland, where those that have been preserved betray a clear relationship to the East. For quite a long time the type with a clothed figure of Christ prevailed. The Germans tried to demonstrate the cosmic significance of the redemption by means of exotic symbols. On a seventh-century gravestone from Faha, now in the Landesmuseum at Trier, the exotic shape of a tau-cross has been converted into the world-embracing figure of Christ crucified.

On the stele from Moselkern, which dates from the end of the seventh century and is now in the Rhein Landesmuseum at Bonn, the figure of Christ is subordinated to a Greek cross. The sun-like head is surrounded by three crosses as though by a halo. The cross of Christ stands above the diagonal world-cross (see illustration 41).

Faha

Carolingian art created truly great pictures of the crucifixion on the smallest scale in ivory. In the middle Christ hangs on the tree of life which once stood in paradise and, according to the legend, provided the wood of the cross. Thus, across the millennia, the relationship between Adam, humanity's first head, and Christ, the new head of the redeemed, is established. Round the trunk is coiled the serpent; it darts its tongue at the vulnerable heel of him who crushed its head by his death. The Church catches the redemptive blood in the chalice, the Synagogue turns away from salvation. Mary and John are present as representatives of believing humanity. Above, angels hover round the cross in adoration, from the depths rise the dead, first-fruits of the redemption. Down below are Gaa and Oceanus, the personification of earth and sea; above, the sun and moon as witnesses of the events. From the clouds the Father's hand stretches out to the Son, to help him or give him the victor's crown. Christ's redemptive act is the centre of cosmic events.

The crucifixion on the so-called votive comb of St Heribert, which dates from the second half of the ninth century, simplifies and condenses the lofty theme into an unforgettable subject for meditation. A rich stylized acanthus and rosette design symbolizes the heavenly paradise, which man lost and the God-man wins back. Angels bend down from it in reverent adoration of the cross. The sun and moon are in mourning. Kneeling, humbly conscious of what they are doing, the soldiers fulfil the old prophecies. Mary and John express their compassion for the crucified Christ so strongly with face and hands and their whole bodies that they already point clearly ahead to Ottonian art.

The series comes to an end about 900 with the diptych of Rambona. The Roman she-wolf has lain down under the cross, which grows vigorously out of the hill like the German tree of life (see illustration 45). Christ's arms embrace the creation with down-turned hands. The old gods are dead. Their pictures above the cross can only symbolize the creation for a little while longer. Mary and John represent the Church, as always in succeeding centuries. Above, two angels carry the half-length portrait of the transfigured Christ, as once two genii bore the picture of the emperor. Popular art has barbarized the classical forms, but also filled them with more vigorous life and cleared the way for future developments.

CHAPTER VI

BYZANTIUM

"Early Byzantine art" is a wide and hardly intelligible concept. It describes the art of the new capital, which between 330 and the death of Justinian in 565 developed the widely varying modes of expression of the imperial territories into the uniform, brilliant imperial style. Its broad foundation was the art of imperial Rome, which itself had moulded the abundant artistic wealth of the subject peoples into something essentially Roman. This Roman style is most easily recognizable in its monumental architecture, huge buildings with plain, massively articulated exteriors, and the structural system hidden in thick walls or supporting subsidiary buildings. Inside there were vast, boldly vaulted spaces of great variety, central spaces with exedrae attached to them, walls articulated by arcades, and much else that the architects of Hagia Sophia were able to put to good use. New Rome learnt its architecture from old Rome. So much is demonstrated by the ruins of Rome, which even today leave such an impression of calm, order and greatness. When the buildings were still undamaged the differences were more apparent. The Romans covered the core of the walls with splendid marble pillars and pilasters, architraves and friezes, in order to make the construction and articulation visible. The Byzantines lightened the smooth walls with flat decorations and thus created their unearthly halls of light. The technique of mosaic-work, too, was taken over from Rome. In the artistic style there is more obvious syncretism. Fifty-seven provinces, of which Rome was only one, were on terms of exchange with Byzantium. The Greek element grows more and more explicit. That is evident from the fact that the Greek language soon ousted Latin from the shores of the Bosphorus. Like all Greek cities, Byzantium always preserved close relations with the Mother-country, even in art. The Greek feeling for the beauty of the human form and for subtlety of line and colour never disappears. Byzantine art never goes back to nature, but always to the naturalistic Greco-Roman inheritance. It preserves classical beauty of form for 1000 years, until it is in danger of ossifying. It rescues Greek art and at the same time ends its classical period, for it also adopts the anti-classical tendencies of the Eastern races. From them it learns the art of strict stylization, of symmetrical construction in different scales according to the significance of the individual figure, and the separation of the three-dimensional space. Through this loss in closeness to life and in surroundings, pictures of the saints gain an arresting immediacy and exaltation above time and place, a solemn dignity and spirituality. These artistic principles were not discovered at Byzantium; they can already be recognized at Dura-Europos. From the fifth century onwards Byzantium was more and more strongly influenced by the wall-decoration, weaving, ceramics and metal-work of the Persian empire. According to Grabar, it took over most of its iconographical themes from Rome and Palestine, but out of all this it created one of the highest syntheses that art has ever accomplished. Its unity is based largely on the fact that it was extensively utilized and guided by the emperor and the Church. It reflects the ideals of the higher civil service and the hierarchy.

It is sad that the wealth of early Byzantine mosaics, except for the remains in Hagia Sophia, Justinian's church on Sinai and a mausoleum in the great oasis were destroyed by the Mohammedans. An idea of the mosaics of Constantinople can best be gained from the church of St George at Salonica, erected by Theodosius out of the huge funeral rotunda of Galerius. In the dome, the angelic host did homage to Christ the victor, who carried the cross like a standard on his shoulder. On the partly preserved frieze below the dome saints stand in front of the palaces of the heavenly Jerusalem. They have faces of Greek beauty and stand in the attitude of Orantes beside those bearing the gospel or the jewelled cross.

BUILDINGS ON A CENTRALIZED PLAN

As we have seen, small martyria could grow into big churches. This happened all the more easily because, from the start, alongside the basilica there were also big centralized buildings for divine service. They mingle with the basilica and finally oust it in the East. Two main kinds can be distinguished. The first develops from the vaulted round space, the second from the square building with four supports. Both have their origin in the East, where the dome has a long history. The Assyrians gave it a more monumental character, and the Persians frequently put it over a square building. It achieved its greatest effect—still visible today in the Pantheon—in its simplest and technically strongest form, as the vault of a strong cylindrical wall, in Roman tombs, temples and baths. The niches in the thick walls gradually became bigger, and went further outwards. Finally they joined up to form a colonnade divided by a ring of columns or pillars from the central space.

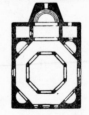

If the octagon was chosen instead of the circle, the building gained stronger accents and firm axes. It could more easily be orientated. Small protruding niches led, over the eight corners, into the dome. The East soon invented pendentives, spherical triangles as

Ezra

bridges between straight walls and round domes. Only small-scale examples are extant. The Romans developed these forms to their furthest extent, employed them on a large scale, brought

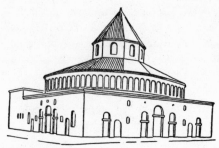

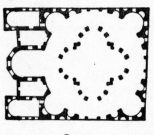

Bosra

them back to the East and with them built the stone symbols of their power and organization. The round building with niches or a low ambulatory remained obligatory in the fourth century for mausolea in both East and West. The more complicated plan of the tall octagon with a two-storeyed ambulatory was employed in 331 for the imperial court church — Constantine's triumphal church—at Antioch. Colonnades formed four semicircular and four right-angled niches between the columns. An entrance hall and apse emphasized the west–east axis. Pillared halls provided a holy precinct round the church. The domed church built of hewn stone, with ambulatory and galleries, which Gregory of Nazianzen mentions in the funeral oration in honour of his father, the builder, was certainly influenced by this first imperial church. Theodosian's court church in the Hebdomon palace copied the prototype at Antioch. In 515 the church of St Gregory at Ezra in Syria was consecrated. Here we have the octagon, without galleries, in a square ambulatory; it is a plain building with clean lines. In 512 the cathedral church at Bosra was built. It has one of the most inspired ground-plans ever conceived. By a cunning

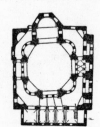

Sergius and Bacchus

system of niches the square of the low outside wall is led amazingly smoothly into the circle of the two-storeyed ambulatory. Out of it rises like a tower the octagon which was once covered with either a conical roof or a wooden dome. These two churches may have been influenced by Byzantium, which took over the lead about this time. The plan of Esra, an octagon in a rectangle, appears in 527 in a more complete form in the church of St Sergius and St Bacchus erected by Justinian and Theodora in the Hormisda palace. Here again, as at Antioch, the niches on the axes were right-angled, and the diagonal ones round. On the ground floor their pillars carry architraves. The longitudinal axis is emphasized by a portico and a spacious apse. The central space, which measures about 40 feet across, is not too high, so that the proportions are broad and harmonious. The umbrella-shaped dome preserves the character of the vigorous pillared construction. Over the upper walls eight shallow arches rise without a break, and over the corners are eight ribs, which bend out so as to bridge the angles. It is a perfect building, combining grace and vigour. It was copied with steeper proportions but the same bulging, rounded niches, by Bishop Ecclesius at Ravenna between 538 and 547. The partly preserved mosaics of San Vitale give some idea of the splendid interior decorations which once enlivened the churches of Constantinople.

Musmieh

Charlemagne followed the tradition of the imperial church when he built the Palatine chapel at Aachen. The tradition comes to an end in the eleventh century at Ottmarsheim on the upper Rhine, where the conventual church is a simplified imitation of Aachen cathedral.

The best-known western octagonal church with ambulatory and apse was the Daurade at Toulouse, a church of Our Lady mentioned by Gregory of Tours in 584. The second group of

Bagaran

large centralized buildings developed from the building with four main supports. Even in the case of octagons on a square foundation, it is dubious whether they grew out of round buildings or square buildings with four supports. In the Near East there had long existed rectangular buildings articulated by four supports. Arches made them into very artistic constructions. The raised square in the middle was covered by a dome or a tent-shaped roof. The four wings had barrel-vaults facing the middle and formed a static counterbalance to it. The four corner-spaces reflected the dome theme on a small scale. Romano-Hellenistic architecture created a perfect example of this in the second-century Tychaeum at Musmieh in Syria (see illustration 9). It was converted into a church in the fourth century. Many martyria and parish churches in the East are based on this form. A sixth-century Christian site, the grave of Aaron, has been distinguished in an Islamic sanctuary on Mount Hor, to the south of the Dead Sea. The tomb-building inside, a rectangle 47 feet by 40, is surrounded by a colonnade and the pilgrims' hospice in the south. It is a building with four supports. The burial church of Rusafa in Mesopotamia, which dates from 575, is a repetition of Musmieh. This form of construction was perfected in Armenia, whose martyria and churches were built in close connection with those of Syria and Palestine and were named after appearances of God in those lands; for example, Etschmiadzin = descent of the only-begotten (*c.* 500). Even here we find many variations of the four-

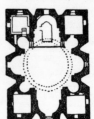

Wagarschapat

support building. The axes are widened into transepts and rounded off with apses. In the cathedral of Bagaran (624) the weighty central tower with a tent-roof over the cupola has assumed a dominating position. The exterior of the church of St Ripsime at Wagarschapat (618) is a typical example of these splendid centralized churches. Inside the eight supports have merged into the walls of the niches. Even if Armenia did not have the influence on Europe which Strzygowski ascribed to it, it developed an individual style of great compactness. In addition, it produced architectural sculpture which points forward in an amazing way to the Romanesque church façades of southern France, northern Italy and South Germany.

THE DOMED BASILICA

Still more important than the pure centralized building is its alliance with the basilica and the subsequent transformation of this mixture into the longitudinal domed church. During the fifth century, in the lands at the eastern end of the Mediterranean, the nave of the galleried basilica was given a light-shaft in front of the apse. A rectangle or square was picked out with pillars, raised above the galleries by the addition of a third storey, and covered with a tent-roof or wooden dome. Either the influence of the martyrium or special circumstances may have been contributory factors. Thus the church of the Virgin of the Spring at Constantinople had the light-shaft over the pool of water. The church on the Ilissos at Athens is reckoned to be the oldest example of the domed basilica.

We are more precisely acquainted with the construction of the church of Alahan Monastir in Isauria, formerly known as Koja Kalessi, which dates

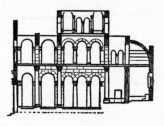

Alahan Monastir

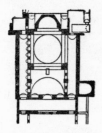

Meriamlik

from some time after 450. In the western part two pairs of columns with pillars placed in front of them support transverse arches, on which lie slabs of stone. After this short yoke comes a big rectangle. Between the columns at its corners stand three pillared arcades on the ground floor, with three more on the top of them in the galleries. Over these are the smaller arcades of a third storey in the shape of a tower. At its corners four arches carried on small pillars lead into an octagon, on which rested the tent-roof or dome.

At Meriamlik in Cilicia a further step forward was taken before 500. The rectangle was replaced by a square. It is more or less certain that there was a dome over this, with a semi-vault over the nave instead of a flat ceiling. The triple choir is pushed up close to the square under the dome. The side-aisles are roofed with semi-barrel-vaults, in order to withstand the pressure of the dome. The whole building is more tightly concentrated on the raised centre. It is dubious whether it should be regarded as a shortened basilica or a lengthened central building.

THE CHURCH WITH A LONGITUDINAL AXIS AND A CENTRAL DOME

The church of Our Lady at Ephesus, built in 550, puts the dome in the central position and counterbalances it in the natural way with big longitudinal barrel-vaults in the nave and small ones in the side-aisles and galleries. There is still a dichotomy. The dome seems to interrupt the nave rather than to bind the whole building together. The perfect solution was found in the church of Irene at Constantinople. Here the dome on its heavy pillars forms the central baldachin, and four barrel-vaults radiate from it in the shape of a cross.

The eastern and western ones are
lengthened a little to make room
for the congregation and to empha-
size the centrifugal character of the
church. The north and south sides
were originally divided off by
columns, even above the galleries.
The church is not far from Hagia
Sophia. It was built at the same time
and forms, as it were, the stage pre-
ceding it. Instead of the eastern and
western vaults, the great imperial
church has semi-domes leading into
the central baldachin. That is the

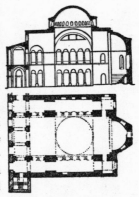

The church of Irene

main reason for the unique effect it produces. The church of
Irene was later rebuilt; the narthex was made part of the nave
and this lengthened western end was covered with a transverse
elliptical dome, to the great disadvantage of the total effect.

Hagia Sophia at Salonica (550) moves the two-storeyed
arcaded wall with the line of windows above back to the outer
wall in the transept. This is a perfect solution for smaller
churches. It is, in fact, the four-columned building of Musmieh
without the four small corner domes. The later cruciform
domed church was to have these as well.

HAGIA SOPHIA

Where Constantine's "great church" had stood, which was
set on fire in 393 when St John Chrysostom was driven out and
was followed by a five-aisled basilica which itself was burnt
down in 532, Anthemios of Tralles and Isidorus of Miletus
built in five years (532–7) Hagia (or Sancta) Sophia, the church
of the Divine Wisdom and one of the wonders of the world. The
perfect combination of centrifugal and centripetal church
which the East was always striving after is here achieved in a

unique way. The path to the altar began once in the atrium at
the west end, where two pillars alternated with one column.
Mosaics and marble, with their changing light and shadow,
gave a foretaste of the interior of the church. The eastern half
of the atrium has been retained as an outer narthex or portico.
The entrances to it are not on the same axis as those to the
inner portico. Thus the path to the altar is
blocked. In the wide inner narthex the
marble-covered east wall forms one last
impressive barrier. There are no architectural divisions in it at all. The arcaded
arches of the cross-vault disappear into it
and are carried on the west side on huge
columns. The giant wall is like a last silence

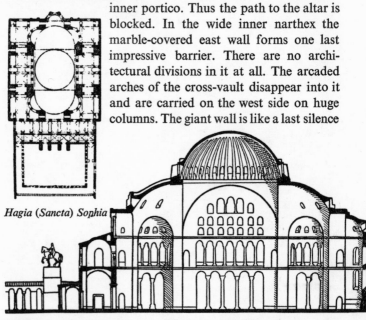

Hagia (Sancta) Sophia

before the interior speaks. Three imperial doors in the
middle and three more on each side of them lead into the
"hall of light that produces its own radiance" (Prokop). Its
arrangement is clear and orderly, like that of Roman buildings,
but less obvious, more mysterious. The Romans had never
hidden the fact that their buildings were composed of great
masses. The controlled mass became the expression of strength,
confidence and duration. Here, too, mighty piers carry the four
arches of the central square. The four corners are rounded at

the top into spherical triangles, pendentives, as they are called. They merge into a closed circle, and this carries the weight of the huge dome, which is over 100 feet wide and 70 feet high. But there is no feeling of weight or mass (see illustration 27).

Above the bright band of forty windows the dome seems to hover like a sky rather than to press down. The huge columns stand out only a little from the wall; they are covered by the same decoration and seem like part of the wall. The arches are not emphasized either. On the long north and south sides they disclose only a little of their breadth inside; outside they form deep caverns of shadow. In the east and west the arches run straight into the semi-domes which convert the central space into a longitudinal one. Each end finishes—on an absolute cascade of domes—in three apses with small semi-domes. Strengthened by two piers, they form the support system of these sides, while in the north and south the pressure of the domes is led away from the middle piers on to the equally strong neighbouring columns by two buttresses in the arches of the ground-floor and galleries, and a third one over the roof. The size of the piers is concealed from view in the ambulatories. The ugly supporting walls on all four sides of the exterior were added between the thirteenth and fifteenth centuries because of the danger of collapse through earthquakes.

In spite of its almost square ground-plan the church is a centrifugal building. The arcades of the north and south walls lead the glance into the depths, in the same way as the protruding barriers of the altar area with the ambo in front had once done. The space runs towards the apses, but its movement is arrested by the peaceful centre. The side-aisles and galleries form a mysteriously twilit casing. Their individual sections do not merge into unity, but turn in continually fresh perspectives to the main area of the building. Over the coloured pillars, which were supplied by the provincial governors, at Justinian's command, from marble quarries and pagan temples, the arches, which can never be seen in their entirety, rise like dark, shadowy trees. It is like looking from a forest on to a beautiful clearing. The facing of the walls heightens this impression. Below, it consists of prophyry, choice slabs of dark green, grey and brownish-red. In the upper ambulatory there is a light grey. Decorative patterns in filigree cover the capitals, mosaics with an edging and flowers the cross- and barrel-vaults. These Persian-inspired decorations cause the individual architectural details to lose definition, so that Paulus Silentiarius felt as though he were looking on the loveliest landscapes of Thessaly, "sprouting corn and thick woods, olive-trees with double trunks and green vines . . . or the peaceful blue of the summer sea".

Above, over this idealized picture of the earth, rests heaven, the home of the holy. All the curved surfaces of the central area once shimmered with gold mosaics. At the apex a jewelled cross shone against a background of stars. When the dome collapsed in the earthquake of 575, Isidore of Miletus' nephew rebuilt it 22 feet higher, thus reducing the horizontal thrust. It contained the picture of the Almighty, the ancient of days, Father and Son in one, lord of the world, judge, protector and teacher. Angels, as the leaders of the heavenly hosts, stood round the Deity at the four points of the compass (Apoc. 7. 1). Below was a circle of apostles and prophets, and in the four corners the evangelists, who link heaven and earth with their tidings.

The interior is not clearly illuminated like Roman buildings, such as the Pantheon. The strongest direct light comes from the edges of the dome and the semi-domes, and falls obliquely. It gives the gold mosaics above a sort of twilight radiance, and at every hour of the day forms paths of light which link continually changing parts of the interior. A weaker light enters through the heavily barred windows above the galleries of the north and south walls, and indirect light comes from the ambulatories. The result is a loss of definition and the disappearance of sharp divisions. Paulus Silentiarius was impressed most by the illumination at night. He describes the garlands and crosses and the silver lamps, which, like ships, "float through the bright paths of the air instead of the waves of the sea".

The ripples of the marble floor fitted in well with this picture. A balustrade of chased silver enclosed the altar-space. The golden altar gleamed with jewels and enamel. Over it rose a baldachin covered by a great golden cross. The celebration of the liturgy was not so much the redemptive sacrifice of Christ the mediator as adoration of the enthroned Lord, whose presence was shown in the picture in the dome. After the most circumstantial and solemn ceremonial, carried out by innumerable dignitaries and six hundred clergy, the royal personages entered and the liturgy reached its consummation. The lofty position of the priest-emperor became visible to all when he passed through the altar-rails to spread the linen over the holy table and incense the crucifixion-group in the apse, when he escorted the offertory gifts to the altar and received holy communion inside the altar-area.

Hagia Sophia, with its picture of the universe in the dome, was the symbol of Christ's government of the world through the emperor; it was the church of Christ, the church of the Divine Wisdom and the palace-church. The emperor was welcomed with chants like those that welcome Christ in the liturgy of Palm Sunday. Important official acts took place here.

THE CHURCH OF THE APOSTLES

Justinian had a new church of the Apostles built, on the site of the old one, by Anthemios of Tralles and the younger Isidore. It did not fall far short of Sancta Sophia. It was a five-domed church with side-aisles and galleries; the ground-plan was a Greek cross. The central dome was raised a little higher than the others by a cylinder, and was lit by windows. It formed the baldachin over the high altar. The gold mosaic showed the Almighty on the rainbow. The eastern dome contained a picture of the crucifixion, the northern and southern ones the transfiguration and the ascension, and the western one the miracle of Pentecost. This grandiose building was destroyed by the Turks. St Mark's at Venice and St Front at Périgueux give some idea of what it must have looked like inside, except that one must add in imagination the atrium, the gallery-colonnades and the altar at the central intersection.

The church of the Apostles served as model for Justinian's church of St John at Ephesus. We have been enabled to reconstruct the plan of this church, and also that of the uncompleted earlier one, by new, careful excavations on the hill of Ajasoluk. A level site was created for the huge new building, which was over 450 feet long, by building up the hill. The atrium with its fountain began on the lofty supporting wall at the western end, and could therefore only be entered from the south. The wide porch of the church, with its five small domes, struck the note for the interior. The ground-plan was extended into a Latin cross by a sixth dome at the west end. The result of this lengthening was that the five domes of the centre only came into view gradually, and thus achieved a greater effect. In place of the old mausoleum, which had blocked the view into the transepts, a baldachin carried on pillars rose over the apostle's grave. The altar-space over the grave was raised a few steps and enclosed by rails. On its east side rose the semicircular benches for the clergy, with the bishop's throne in the middle. The big drums for the pillars of the dome and the marble for the walls were provided by the temple of Diana—built in the seventh century before Christ and one of the seven wonders of the ancient world—in front of which Demetrius the silversmith incited the people to attack Paul. Three beautiful slabs from the temple of Diana also found a home at this time in the altar-area of the church of St Catherine at the foot of Mount Sinai. All the vaulted ceilings of the church of St John were covered with paintings or mosaics. The result must have been a

wonderful symphony of colour and forms. The weight of the
arches was dispersed in a trellis of pillars, and the whole
interior was protected from profanation by a two-storeyed
screen. It was not so much the
domes as the intermingling of
nave and transepts
which was impor-

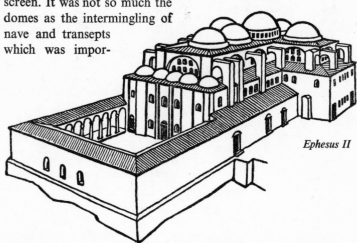

Ephesus II

tant for the future. In 1304 the Seljuks converted this pilgrimage church into a mosque, and later into a market. It was
completely destroyed by an earthquake.

THE CRUCIFORM DOMED CHURCH

The age of Justinian created ideal interiors. Round a broad
central space the apses and ambulatories lie in harmonious
interconnection like a protective envelope or sheath. Afterwards everything grew harsher and more compressed. The
heavy blows suffered by the empire after Justinian's death may
have contributed to this. This great ruler had once more pushed
out the frontiers of the empire as far as Cordoba in Spain and
Nisibis in Mesopotamia, but his successors could not hold
what he had won. The Slavs broke into Greece, and the
Lombards into Italy. Heraclius (610–17) won a great deal

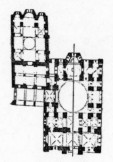

Hosios Lukas

back, but from its new capital, Damascus, Islam soon held sway over Persia,
Syria, Palestine and Egypt. In the
churches built at that time massive
piers obstruct the interior, emphasizing
the cruciform shape and the path to the
altar. One single style replaces the previous variety. It is the cruciform domed
church on a rectangular ground-plan,
with the intersection of the vaults and
the main dome in the middle, and
subsidiary domes over the corners. It
is in fact the plan of the second-century Praetorium at
Musmieh. All five domes are raised on a tambour; this makes
the proportions still narrower. They become wider with
the transition to eight supports, which make bigger domes
possible. The best example of this kind of church is Hosios
Lukas in Greece, with its splendid mosaics (beginning of the
eleventh century). The Balkans and Persia built their churches
on this plan for many centuries.

CHAPTER VII

RAVENNA

Only in the magic city of Ravenna, which was dependent on Byzantium culturally, and later politically as well, can we still see basilica and centrifugal church, baptistery and martyrium, in the glory of the old mosaics. Twenty churches are fairly well preserved, and we know the names of thirty more that have perished.

When Theodosius the Great died in 395, his sons shared the empire. Arcadius took over the East with Constantinople as his capital; Honorius took the West with Milan. Seven years later, hard pressed by the Visigoths under Alaric, he moved his capital to Ravenna, which was protected by marshes. In the time of Honorius himself, Bishop Ursus built the five-aisled cathedral, which was reminiscent of the chief church of Jerusalem by virtue of its circular shrine in the crypt and its name Anastasis (Resurrection). After his death in 423, his half-sister Galla Placidia ruled until 450 on behalf of her son, Valentinian. She had been raped at Rome and had married Alaric's successor; after his murder she married one of his generals. Her name is linked for ever with the older buildings: San Giovanni Evangelista, Santa Agata, the Baptistery of the Orthodox and, above all, with the so-called

MAUSOLEUM OF GALLA PLACIDIA

This stood at the narthex of the palace church of Santa Croce. In reality it was a shrine in honour of St Laurence, veneration for whom had been encouraged by St Ambrose. It is a plain brick building in the style of the martyria of Asia Minor. The four barrel-vaulted arms of a cross meet in the raised central space, whose dome is concealed on the outside by a pyramid roof.

Slabs of honey-coloured alabaster admit a muted light through small windows. Against the dark blue background of the dome the cross glitters in the centre of concentric circles of stars. It is the sky in the nocturnal darkness of the earthly veil which precedes eternal day. In the corners are the four beings, on each of the four perpendicular walls two apostles, praying, in white garments, against the green background of paradise. The remaining four apostles are depicted on the vaults of the eastern and western arms of the cross. In the lunette of the front arm of the cross, and therefore in the spot most easily visible to those entering the building, Laurence hastens towards the martyrium, with the gospel in his hand and the cross, the symbol of victory, on his shoulder. To the left of the glowing grating stands a big chest holding the gospels: "Evangelium Christi, unde martyres fiunt", as St Cyprian says: "the Gospel of Christ creates martyrs". The picture of the arch-martyr is placed over the spot where the martyr's grave usually is. It takes the place of relics. For this reason the building is closely related to martyria. In the northern lunette, over the entrance and opposite the picture of Laurence, is the last and loveliest picture of the Good Shepherd produced by ancient art. Christ sits as a royal shepherd in a gold-embroidered tunic and purple cloak, his raised left hand resting on the cross as if on a

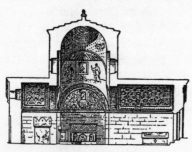

Chapel of Galla Placidia

sceptre, in an idealized landscape with six sheep round him, one of which he is caressing. "No one shall snatch them from my hand." This is the faith that enables Laurence to conquer death.

THE BAPTISTERY OF THE ORTHODOX

San Giovanni in Fonte was built between 449 and 458 by Bishop Neon. Its mosaics are the best preserved. It is an octagonal building, with a hanging dome resting on the eight semicircular arches of the walls, which are lit by big windows, articulated by small pillars and adorned with tendrils. At the apex of the dome, over the font, there is a picture of the baptism of Christ with the dove hovering over him and a personification of the Jordan. Baptism is entry into the kingdom of God, endowment with citizenship; it confers the right

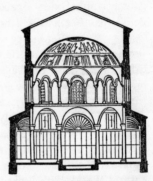

Baptistery of the Orthodox

to a place in the heavenly mansions. So at Christ's baptism heaven has opened its gates. The twelve apostles, as agents of salvation, the highest officials of the kingdom of heaven, bring Christ golden crowns on veiled hands. The next circle shows the architecture of the city of God, built of gold and precious stones. There are eight separate pieces of architecture, each with three niches. Four of the central niches contain an altar with opened gospels, the other four show the throne standing ready with cross and purple cushion. These pictures symbolize the fact that in baptism Christ makes his followers into kings and priests.

The eight big aisles of the window area and the mosaics of the lowest circle complete the picture of paradise with their vine-tendrils and peacocks. Beside the windows there are low reliefs of the sixteen prophets—the foundation of the city of

God—and among the tendrils of the ground floor there are eight saints. A magnificent theology of baptism is thus expounded in a relatively small space.

In 476 the West Roman Empire came to an end. Theodoric and the Ostrogoths marched down from the Balkans on Odoacer, who had declared himself independent of Byzantium in 486. In 493 Theodoric captured Ravenna; from there he ruled Italy until 526. He was succeeded by his daughter Amalaswintha, who reigned until Ravenna was taken in 540 by Belisarius, Justinian's general. Under the rule of the Arian Ostrogoths the Baptistery of the Arians was built about 500, on similar lines to that of the Orthodox. Once again the apostles, led by Peter with the keys and Paul with two papyrus rolls, bring their crowns to the *etimasia*, the throne of the ruler of the world, on which stands the jewelled cross, the symbol of Christ. There is a noticeably greater departure from ancient art. The use of tendrils, candelabra and niches as divisions is abandoned, and the movement of the apostles is calmer. They stand large and isolated in the pure golden light of the supernatural world. The limitation to essentials brings a gain in composure.

The archiepiscopal chapel, a little jewel, with a picture of Christ the Emperor in the portico, was built a little later (see illustration 25). About 500, too, Theodoric began to build his palace-church, known since the ninth century as San Apollinare Nuovo. In the eighth century its apse was almost completely destroyed by an earthquake. So one must transfer in imagination the apse-mosaic of San Apollinare in Classe, where the mosaics in the nave are missing, in order to have a complete picture of what an old basilica looked like.

SAN APOLLINARE NUOVO

The nave-walls of the palace church still enable us to understand even today why, when this Arian church was consecrated for Catholic worship by Archbishop Agnellus (557–70), it received the title of St Martin-in-the-Golden-Heaven. Nowhere else has the significance of the basilica as a centrifugal church leading up to the altar and as heavenly throne-room been made so clear by its pictorial decoration. Those who enter the church find themselves transported into a solemn scene of homage, a heavenly audience. Over the arcades, divorced from all contact with earth, a long procession of martyrs, led by St Martin, moves from the palace of Theodoric to Christ on his throne, bringing him their crowns of honour. On the left, the north side, a procession of women martyrs, led by the three kings, walks from the port of Classis towards Mary, enthroned with the Christ-child. Four angels stand by. In the same way the senators of Rome and Constantinople used to bring a garland of honour to the emperor, as a drawing from the base of Arcadius' column at Constantinople shows. The martyrs testify that only through the struggle of Christ could they achieve their victory. The female martyrs, in tunics, dalmatics and gold-embroidered togas, resemble patrician ladies doing homage to the newly crowned empress. The most charming is Agnes. She alone is given the Lamb as attribute, just as on the other side the highly honoured Laurence wears a gold-embroidered tunic under the pallium and brings a kind of imperial crown to Christ. The Arians, who denied the divinity of Christ, had found no difficulty in letting the "Mother of God" keep her full royal dignity. She sits on a star-decked cushion, which indicates her cosmic significance in the scheme of salvation. The processions of martyrs were probably remodelled in the time of Archbishop Agnellus. The inspired grace of these women and the humble dignity of the men are surpassed by the expressiveness given to the men of God in the zone above. Here, between the windows, stand thirty-two prophets, apostles and evangelists, not distinguished as such but all identified by the roll of manuscript or the holy book as bearers and heralds of salvation. The variations on this somewhat narrow theme are amazingly rich. All these figures are men possessed by God, seers and sages summoning the community of the faithful, but each in a different way corresponding to the character and age of the individual. Vanishing antiquity's noblest ideal of humanity is here elevated into the Christian picture of man. In the highest zone there is a baldachin over each of these inspired figures, with a crown hanging in it and the cross between two doves standing on it. Between the baldachins, over the windows, are pictures of Christ by other artists. Unfortunately rather small in size, they are well known from reproductions. On the north wall above the female martyrs, these pictures consist of thirteen scenes from the life of Christ, of the sort to be found in the collections of Sunday gospels popular at that time, the so-called perikope books. Under these are a number of previously seldom or never employed themes, such as the calling of Peter and Andrew, Pharisees and publicans, and the widow's mite. On the north wall there are thirteen pictures of Our Lord's passion, from the Last Supper to the appearance before Thomas. The intention is to show the glorification of the Son of God through his sacrifice. For this reason Christ prays on the Mount of Olives in the solemn attitude of a suppliant, in the midst of the apostles. Christ carries the cross like a battle-standard, and there is no picture of the crucifixion itself.

SAN APOLLINARE IN CLASSE

The building of San Vitale was financed by the patrician Julianus Argentarius. At the same time he built at the port of Classe a basilica in honour of the city's patron saint. Today the church stands on its own in the fields some distance from the sea (see illustration 23). The differences from the Roman basilica are obvious. The round bell-tower was built later, in the eighth or ninth century; it copies eastern models. On the other hand, the raising of the narthex like a tower on the north side is old; there was to be a similar tower on the south side, as at Turmalin. The pastophoria are Syrian, too. The toning-down of the individual parts to assist the impression made by the building as a whole is Byzantine. The cornices are smaller and the arcades broader. The side-aisles have windows and share the bright light of the centre. The walls above the arcades are no longer broken up into sections by pilasters. The picture in the apse makes up for the loss of the mosaics in the nave. It will be discussed in the section on mystery-pictures.

A late seventh-century mosaic on the left-hand wall of the apse reminds us once again of the very close link between State and Church. It shows the solemn transference of privileges to the archbishop of Ravenna, who at that period was for a short time autocephalous, that is, independent of Rome.

The picture opposite is correspondingly more liturgical. In the middle stands the high priest Melchisedech making a sacrifice at the altar. From the left Abel brings a lamb; from the right Abraham leads his son, the prefiguration of Christ, to the altar.

SAN VITALE

San Vitale is yet another example of the splendid centrifugal churches of the eastern empire. Archbishop Ecclesius laid the foundation stone after his return from Byzantium, where he may have been fascinated by the church of St Sergius and St Bacchus. Archbishop Maximian put the domes on the building and consecrated it in 547. No picture can convey the impression received by the visitor who walks round it (see illustration 26). Rich variety combines to produce a felicitous unity. The central space swells out between massive piers into seven semicircular niches with two rows of graceful columns, one on top of the other; the ambulatory forms a protective envelope of twilight. The eighth side opens into the most beautiful choir that can be imagined, a radiant picture of heaven in gold, green and red. In the mystery picture in the apse Christ sits in a purple robe on the blue globe of earth over the four rivers of paradise. In his left hand he holds the scroll with seven seals. The jewelled cross, symbol of the second coming and the lordship of the world, is made into a big halo. Two princely angels stand at his side. The one on the right-hand side leads up the patron saint, Vitalis. With veiled hands he receives his diadem from Christ: the final crowning of the martyr who has given witness with his blood. The other angel is bringing up Bishop Ecclesius with a model of the church. He is still imperfect and therefore has no halo. His consecration-gift and his position as representative of the community opposite the martyr indicate clearly that the Christian's path leads through earthly trial to heavenly coronation.

A broad band over the background of the apse shows motifs from imperial triumphal art. There are seven pairs of crossed cornucopias on each side; on the two top ones are the imperial eagles, which hold on their wing-tips, instead of the image of the emperor, a shield with the monogram of Christ on it.

The cross-vault over the choir is a brightly coloured carpet of tendrils, flowers and animals, especially peacocks, the symbols of immortality. Over the groins wind heavy garlands of flowers, which unite in a garland supported by four angels. In the garland stands the Lamb with a halo, against a blue background studded with stars. The Lamb that was slaughtered is at the same time the Lamb on the mountain to which redeemed creation does homage. The pictures on the side-walls show the prefigurations of Christ: the sacrifices of Abel, Melchisedech and Abraham; the meal taken by the three men with Abraham; and God's appearances to Moses, the mediator between God and his people. Two other famous mosaics on the side-walls form an accompaniment to the celebration of the liturgy. Emperor and archbishop have greeted each other in the portico of the church and are proceeding with their retinue in a solemn procession, behind the deacon with his thurifer, into the church. Justinian is carrying a precious vessel containing a gift of gold coin, Theòdora a chalice. The Church honours the emperor as its protector by granting him this place near the altar; the emperor honours the Church as the community of salvation, of which he is a member. The presentation of gifts is as solemn as the procession of saints. The earthly monarchs know that they represent the monarch of heaven. That is why they are divorced from the earthly and the profane. Their bodies are transformed into immaterial, decorative forms. But the faces and royal insignia are astonishingly true to nature (see illustration 24).

MAXIMIAN'S THRONE

Amongst other things, Archbishop Maximian had the famous ivory chair made, which is today in the cathedral museum. It shows that even at its climax the imperial style only succeeded in unifying the artistic characteristics of the individual races to a limited extent. Panels by different artists and of very different inspiration stand immediately next to each other. The reliefs depicting the story of Joseph on the narrow sides are of Hellenistic charm. They could have been produced in Alexandria. The tendrils and pictures on the front are very un-Greek. They are Syrian in spirit. The tendrils and animals could be patterns for Romanesque capitals, and the four evangelists and John the Baptist point forward to the sculptures of Bamberg and Strasbourg.

CHAPTER VIII

MYSTERY AND CULT PICTURES

The oldest, hastily painted Christian pictures, with their symbol of the shepherd and teacher, aimed at directing attention to the redemption and the new life in Christ. They had no reference to worship. But when pictures entered the church and occupied the important position in the apse the idea arose of harnessing them to the ritual. When, in the Mass, the mystery of Christ's redemptive act, of his death, resurrection and glorification was mysteriously renewed, it seemed desirable to put it before the faithful in visible form in the apse-picture. The idea had already been put into effect on a magnificent scale in St John Lateran. It was repeated in a more strictly symbolical fashion about 400 in the tripartite apse of the basilica of Felix at Nola. Paulinus' descriptive poem allows us to reconstruct the mosaic with some certainty (see the drawing on p. 139).

NOLA

In the clouds appears the hand of the Father. From him goes Christ as mediator through the spirit of love down to the lower sphere. This is at the same time both earthly and eschatological. The Lamb stands as if slaughtered and at the same time worshipped by the twelve lambs. Seen from below, the jewelled cross no longer signifies Christ's departure from glory, but his return to it; the twelve apostles form his halo. The cross occupies the centre, as the head and shoulders of Christ do at the Lateran.

S. PUDENZIANA

The oldest big apse-picture that has been preserved is in the relatively small church of S. Pudenziana, which was built about 400. The picture was restored in the eighth and sixteenth

Nola

centuries and severely trimmed all round; in 1830 it was somewhat infelicitously completed by Nazarenes. However, the general effect can still be appreciated (see illustration 20). Christ sits as a teacher, like one of the ancient philosophers, indeed almost like Jupiter, in the midst of all the apostles. The female figures of the Jewish and gentile churches bring the golden wreath of homage by way of thanks for the redemption, which is recalled by the cross on Golgotha, outlined in the background in front of the buildings of Jerusalem. At the same time Christ is enthroned on a purple cushion adorned with precious stones in the midst of the four huge beings of the Apocalypse. The cross on Golgotha, being a jewelled cross, is a symbol of the glorification of Christ and of the second coming. The earthly Jerusalem becomes a picture of the heavenly one. The historical act of salvation and the final glorification were depicted yet again on the lower strip, which has been cut off. In it the Lamb stood on the mountain of paradise, with the twelve lambs coming to him. Over that was the dove of the spirit. When in the liturgy the historical coming of Christ was recalled and his final coming promised, it was as if a curtain had been pushed aside and the faithful could see with their own eyes what was being invisibly carried out in the mystery of the Mass.

SAN AQUILINO

A mosaic from the middle of the fifth century has been preserved in the chapel of San Aquilino beside the church of San Lorenzo at Milan. The apostles' teacher, of whom we are reminded by the opened papyrus roll, has become the lofty ruler, surrounded by the twelve in the guise of senators of Christ, judges over the tribes of Israel. As in the Apocalypse, they are dressed, like Christ, as victors, in shining white linen. The pure gold background removes the scene from all contact with earth. The relationship to the liturgy is not so clear in this martyr's chapel as it is in the parish church of SS. Cosma e Damiano.

SS. COSMA E DAMIANO

This church was installed between 526 and 530 in a pagan building in the Forum. This standing figure of Christ at the second coming, dressed in white raiment shimmering with gold, in front of reddish clouds on a deep-blue background, exercises a compulsive power. In his left hand he holds the book of life, with his right he summons all creatures and points to the phoenix, the symbol of immortality (see illustration 21). Above him could once be seen the hand of the Father holding the victor's laurel, below him the Lamb and the twelve sheep. Cosmas and Damian, led by the apostles and half turning to the congregation that they represent, are carrying their crowns to Christ, the first-born of the dead, the ruler over the kings of the earth. St Theodore and the founder, Felix, stand by. Christ is both the Lamb that was slaughtered and the phoenix that rose again. Once again past and future are combined in one. On the badly damaged triumphal arch the Lamb was depicted on the throne, and below the sealed book, the seven lamps, the four living creatures and the elders.

SAN APOLLINARE IN CLASSE

Over the wide paradise landscape gleams the great star-studded gloriole with the jewelled cross, the emblem of the Son of Man. The apocalyptic letters A and O are inscribed on the ends of the cross-beam, *ICHTHYS* and *SALUS MUNDI* on the longitudinal beams. The ninety-nine stars signify the lord of the universe (cosmocrator), the ruler of the world. At the same time it is the transfiguration on Mount Tabor. Moses and Elias appear in the clouds, three lambs looking upwards symbolize Peter, James and John, and the Father's hand is visible above. Cross and glory are brought into relation with each other, for the prophets are talking to Christ about his passion. The patron saint of Ravenna had to be included, in the most striking position, over his grave in the apse. He did not fit into a historical picture of the transfiguration, so the historical event was elevated by the abstract style of its depiction into something timeless and the figure of the saint thus endowed with increased significance. Just as in Palestinian mosaics, which are reflected in the oil-flasks of Monza, Mary

stands amid the apostles under the mandorla[1] of Christ
ascending into heaven, so here Apollinaris stands in the midst
of the twelve lambs. The lambs are not coming from the holy
cities; they signify not the apostles, but the community of
Ravenna. Apollinaris is their shepherd and model. His earthly
passion has led him to the glorified Christ in paradise. There
he is an intercessor for his flock, their shepherd in the name
of Christ. His position as a proxy is made clear in the picture
on the triumphal arch over the apse. Twelve lambs climb up
from the gates of Jerusalem and Bethlehem to Christ, the chief
shepherd. The lambs round Apollinaris form a unity with the
upper ones and are referred by his attitude of prayer to
Christ.

PARENZO IN ISTRIA

Here we find an innovation. The picture resembles that of
San Vitale, but Christ is not enthroned on the globe; instead,
Mary is his living throne, the seat of the logos. When the
domed church was developed in the East, Christ was given the
dominating position in it. The second best position, in the apse,
was given to the Mother of God. In the painters' book of
Mount Athos, which is based on very old sources, we find the
following direction: "If you are going to paint a domed church,
up in the tympanum make a circle and in it paint Christ giving
a blessing and holding the Gospel on his breast, and write this
inscription: Jesus Christ the universal ruler (pantocrator). In
the sanctuary, in the middle of the eastern vault, paint the
Virgin Mary, sitting on a throne and holding Christ as a little
child, and over her write the inscription: Mother of God,
higher than the sky. On each side paint the archangels Michael
and Gabriel."

Parenzo possesses the oldest mosaic designed on this pattern.
Mary is enthroned between the archangels, full of dignity, yet
also very human. On her lap she holds the Christ-child dressed

[1] Almond-shaped aureole surrounding the whole figure (*Tran.*)

in tunic and pallium. Here, too, the old idea is still perfectly clear. The Father's hand can be seen, holding the victor's wreath, the reward for fighting the good fight. Martyrs who, supported by his strength, testified with their blood, bring him their crowns.

Because there is no dome, Christ sits as universal ruler with book and gesture of authority between the apostles on the star-studded wall over the apse. The broad band along the edge of the arch contains twelve medallions on each side of the lamb. Here again we have the whole span of Christ's life from childhood to the end of the Passion, the divine drama of the struggle and victory of Christ and his faithful followers.

In the western churches built under Byzantine influence the pattern laid down by the painters' book was sometimes strictly followed; at Torcello, for example, where the great figure of Mary stands alone in the apse. In other cases a compromise was adopted: a smaller picture of Mary was placed underneath the big head and shoulders of Christ in the apse. This solution was chosen at Cefalu and Monreale. In most churches of the West the old tradition was retained. Thus, for example, in the ninth century, the rich mosaics of S. Prassede follow those of SS. Cosma e Damiano. Two-dimensional, with the emphasis on the outlines, they make a strong appeal to modern taste; in the nineteenth century they were regarded as artistically decadent.

In Carolingian and Ottonian churches, to judge by the titles that have been preserved, Christ in his glory seems to have been almost the only theme of apse-pictures. We can reconstruct the lost pictures from paintings in books, which partly reflected, partly inspired large-scale art. Christ was usually depicted with an almond-shaped halo, surrounded by the four living creatures.

This picture was also a regular feature of Romanesque churches. With the arrival of the Gothic style the mystery-picture loses its representative position; we shall see in due course what it was replaced by.

The mystery-picture in the apse is a natural climax of Christian pictorial art. It illustrates, but at the same time preserves a certain remoteness. It remains clearly recognizable as a symbol, a pointer to a reality which cannot itself be depicted. It does not provoke public or private adoration. Christian art might well have remained content with pictures such as these, and in the West it did. In the East, on the other hand, a fairly clear line of development leads to the cult-picture proper, which is identified much more closely with the saint himself. This development begins quite early with a certain respect for pictures, which later grows into veneration. The traditions in which the newly converted had grown up turned out to be very strong. They were used to portraits of ancestors in places of honour, busts of the dead on sarcophagi, garlanded pictures of famous men, and votive pictures as expressions of thanks to a helpful divinity. It was a short step to transfer all this to a venerated martyr. The blood-witness is united in death to Christ and can therefore guarantee the divine presence more surely. Therefore his relics are held in honour, and, if these are missing, his picture—the depiction of his passion and crowning—as well. People think that they will thereby gain a share in his union with Christ. Especially in the shrines of Palestine the bright golden mosaics represented in a small way Christ and Mary. Copies of them spread everywhere and inspired to devotion those who could not make a pilgrimage.

Considerable stimulus was provided by the effigy of the emperor.

Since in the liturgy, and in the pictures in apses and on sarcophagi, the ritual of emperor-worship was transferred so naturally to the Emperor Christ, it was a short step to transfer the veneration of the emperor's picture to that of Christ. At the beginning of an emperor's reign his effigy was sent even to the most distant provinces, solemnly welcomed, decked with laurel, honoured with genuflections, incense and candles, and carried round in processions. In the latter part of the fourth century the "true picture" of Christ began to receive the same treatment. *Acheiropoieta*, that is, pictures of Christ not painted by human hands, began to appear, and also so-called Abgar-pictures, copies of the impression of Christ's features on a cloth that he was supposed to have sent to Abgar, prince of Edessa, at the latter's request. The theological reasons for and against such pictures were first clearly formulated about 400; they were to be repeated for centuries. Eusebius wrote as follows to Constantine's daughter when he refused her request for a picture of Christ:

If only the Father knows the Son, there can be no true picture of Christ. Certainly not of his divine nature, at any rate. But even his human side, the figure of a young man, is transformed by his unspeakable and indescribable radiance. If Constantia wants a picture of Christ's untransformed human form, that offends against God's commandment not to make images of heavenly or earthly things.

Bishop Epiphanius of Salamis argues on very similar lines: Scripture and tradition forbid pictures. Christ's divinity cannot be portrayed. How can the incomprehensible, unspeakable, unthinkable, uncircumscribable God, whom not even Moses could look upon, be portrayed in paint? And Christ's humanity is so much tinged with God's glory that it cannot be grasped in isolation.

This thought must have made a particular impression on the Monophysites, who saw only one nature in Christ, the divine one. Their opponents, the Nestorians, made too great a division between the two natures. They said that Christ was a human being, in whom divinity dwelt as in a temple. So they renounced pictures, too, because a picture of the purely human side could clearly not be a true picture of Christ. They made an exception for the crucifix, which they did much to popularize, because, in their view, on the cross Christ's divinity had been completely hidden.

Asterius of Amasia writes: "Do not paint pictures of Christ; one humiliation is enough for him, the incarnation, to which he submitted himself for our sake. Carry rather the incorporeal word spiritually in your heart."

Other Fathers of the Church like Basil and Gregory of Nyssa defended pictures as early as the fourth century on grounds which were still adduced by theologians in the great dispute about images in the eighth century:

God in his eternal being, they said, cannot be portrayed, but in Christ he has taken shape. The supernatural has become visible and tangible. Christ is "the true likeness of the God we cannot see" (Col. 1. 15). If God himself makes the bodily form his likeness, it cannot be blasphemous to evoke this living likeness with a painted symbol. The picture reminds us of Christ in the same way as a picture of the king or a friend reminds us of them. Basil was the originator of the formula repeated so often later on: the honour paid to a picture is honour paid to the original of the picture. Dionysius Areopagiticus adds: "Because pictures portray holy and venerable people, they share their honour and humiliation." The legitimization of Christian art by the incarnation of the Logos was thus recognized quite early.

Epiphanius's pronouncement, at first sight so illuminating, has never been clearly refuted. Epiphanius is adopting a Monophysite attitude when he maintains that Christ's divinity shone forth directly from his earthly form, and demands as much from pictures. This is asking too much of Christian art. The solution to the problem was never formulated in so many words at that time, but in practice it was more and more nearly achieved. It consists in depicting Christ's humanity in such a way that its indissoluble union with his divinity is expressed symbolically. Early Christian art is only concerned to hint through painted images at the mystery of God's appearance in the flesh, and thus to confess its belief.

In the fifth century the veneration of pictures was not yet very widespread. In the sixth century there are signs that it was already taken for granted. The prototypes of "holy" pictures were small devotional pictures of Christ or the saints in the corners of churches and crypts, fixed low enough on walls or pillars for people to become familiar with and fond of (see illustration 31). Other small pictures, especially pilgrims' souvenirs, were to be found in private houses. According to Theodoret, at Rome there were small pictures of St Simeon Stylites in every shop and workroom. The oldest picture that can be described as an ikon in the accepted sense of the term is a Madonna in Santa Maria Nuova at Rome which dates from the seventh or eighth century. It has a majestic, soulful countenance with great eyes looking into the next world (see illustration 30). The connection between pictures such as this and the expressive faces of Egyptian mummies has rightly been emphasized. The monastery of Sinai, the only one not stripped of its pictures by the Mohammedans, preserved some ikons of saints painted between the sixth and eighth centuries. In the seventh century holy pictures were to be found all over the eastern empire. They were venerated with obeisance, incense, candles, processions and hymns. The gold of the clothes and backgrounds, and the solemn full-face pose of the subjects made them seem like reflections of heaven. The picture could take the place of the saint; power was ascribed to it. There was a considerable danger of people trying to conjure the supernatural by magic and material objects. The bitter arguments of the great dispute about images in the eighth and ninth centuries were bound to arise sooner or later. The Emperor Leo III began the struggle in 726 with sermons and disputations. He was supported by many bishops and influenced to some extent by the Jews and the Mohammedans. In 730 he issued an edict forbidding the veneration of images. It did not come to persecution and iconoclasm until the reign of his son Constantine V. In 754 the Council of Hieria condemned images on similar grounds to those already advanced by Epiphanius. In 787 the Council of Nicaea permitted the veneration of images, after the regent Irene had with difficulty re-established peace. The second instalment of the struggle, which lasted from 813 to 842, was no less bitter. The patriarch Anastasius was dragged to death. The struggle ended in 843 with the re-erection of images by the Empress-widow Theodora. This was commemorated with a "feast of orthodoxy".

In the first half of the dispute about images the leading defender was John of Damascus, in the second Theodore of Studion. They created the "theology of images" which assured the veneration of Byzantine and Russian ikons for a thousand years. John of Damascus elucidated the position as follows: in a picture, it is not the thing that is worshipped, but the creator of the thing. The picture is a likeness, an imitation of the original, namely Christ's human nature. There is a certain similarity between the picture and the original, not in the substance, but in the person. Because the picture aims at portraying the whole Christ, in whom the two natures are indivisible, it wins a mysterious share in Christ's divinity. It is itself something holy, a sort of visible proxy of the original, not in essence, but in power and grace. Just as the subject of the picture is full of the Holy Ghost, so also is the picture (2 *Homily*, 14). It is a mystery that has something of the sacramental about it. It prolongs the incarnation of God and is a visible reminder to seek the divine, as though through a transparent screen. John of Damascus' main idea, that in the depiction of Christ's humanity the divinity that is indivisibly united with it is also present in proportion to the efficacy of the picture, was violently attacked by his opponents. They said that the union of divine and human natures in Christ was a mystery that God alone could create and that man could not imitate in art. The divine, in its infinity, could in no wise be circumscribed.

Divine and human natures would either be mixed together, as the Monophysites would have them, or completely divided in accordance with Nestorian belief.

At this point Theodore of Studion took up the defence and explained, with the help of Neo-Platonism, how there could after all be some kind of a circumscription. John of Damascus had already noted a gradation of images in history, from the shadowy prototypes of the Old Covenant to the clear images of the New, from Christ the true image of the Father to man as an image and likeness, and he had added at the end the pictures of painters. His opponents had objected that there was a wide gap between the natural images created by God himself and the artistic ones of painters.

Theodore of Studion now showed how the divinity itself creates ever further removed copies of itself and virtually contains all these removes in itself. The last and lowest of these removes, pictures painted by men, belong to the divine original as the shadow does to the body. The painted picture is a last *eksphrágisma* or seal-impression of the divine original.

Thus this theology of pictures, like the ikons which produced it, centres round the mystery of the incarnation. It testifies to the belief in Christ as a copy of the Father in the flesh, and it wishes to evoke this similarity with the means at its disposal. Conversely, pictures are intended to facilitate man's return to his divine original.

The eastern dispute about images also influenced the western Church. Charlemagne's court theologians wrote the *Libri Carolini* in order to combat an inaccurate translation of the proceedings of the Council of Nicaea. They scarcely recognize even the didactic value of pictures. Pictures are material objects, they say, as opposed to the immaterial nature of the divine countenance; they contain no mystery; people who venerate pictures are venerators of colours, worshippers of panels and walls. Pictures are for people with bad memories.

These books were not recognized by the Roman Church. Pope Hadrian I allowed pictures to be venerated as before.

In the West the developments were more peaceful. After long hesitation the Church took pictures into its service because it recognized how helpful to faith and religious life they could be. There are indications that in the West as well pictures were venerated to some extent quite early on. Augustine said anxiously: "I know there are many who venerate graves and pictures." Gregory the Great had to restrain the zeal for destruction of Bishop Serenus of Marseilles: "We have been informed that thoughtless zeal has led you to smash pictures of saints, and that you have excused yourself on the grounds that pictures should not be worshipped. For forbidding their worship you deserve only praise, but for smashing them you must be censured. It is one thing to worship a painting, but another to be reminded by it of its subject. For what writing is to the literate, painting is to the uneducated. Paintings are employed in churches so that the illiterate can at least read by looking at the walls what they cannot read in books." The Carolingian books had little influence. This is shown by Charlemagne's decree of 807, which orders the king's representatives to investigate the condition of churches and their paintings. Furthermore there is the opposition which Bishop Claudius of Milan encountered when he cleared away from the churches of his diocese "the filth of votive gifts and pictures". In the tenth century the schoolman Bernard of Angers complained about the veneration of images in southern France. He is referring more to the big statues first made at that time, which fascinated people with their gold paint. The great expounders of ecclesiastical symbolism like Honorius, Sicardus and Durandus summed up the value of pictures in the brief formula: *Laicorum litteratura*, the literature of the uneducated.

The attitude to pictures varied considerably in different parts of the West. In the north it was their expressive symbolism and educational effect that were valued, in the south it was their gripping immediacy. Thomas Aquinas produced the best summary of the position. He said that pictures could reasonably be employed (1) like books, to instruct the uneducated, (2) to remind people of the mystery of the incarnation and of the example of the saints and (3) to inspire devotion, which arises more easily from what we see than from what we hear. Moreover, following other schoolmen, Thomas also showed, in a wonderful section of his *Summa Theologica*, his understanding of the irrational element in the cult-image and its veneration: When one turns to an image, he says, in so far as it is a thing— either a painting or a statue—it deserves no veneration. But if one turns to it as an image of Christ, it deserves the same reverence as Christ himself. "Since Christ is worshipped with humble veneration, it follows that his image, too, must be worshipped with (relatively) humble veneration" (*Summa Theol.* III, qu. 25, art. 3).

PICTURES OF THE TRINITY

Pictures of the Trinity deserve a separate mention, for they can only occasionally be classified as mystery-pictures and almost never as cult-images. The first pictures of the Trinity are baptismal scenes. Christ's divinity is attested by the Father's hand and the dove flying down. The older mystery-pictures are at the same time pictures of the Trinity. The later ones sometimes lack the hand or the dove and thus the trinitarian aspect, which was transferred quite early on to the *etimasia*,[1] the "ready throne". Since the time of Alexander the Great a gilded throne with a golden crown lying on it could represent the ruler. At Christian councils the throne with the Gospel on it represented Christ. In mosaics, the throne, as described by St John in the fourth chapter of the Apocalypse, stands for the Father. On the throne lies the Gospel, the cross or the Lamb.

[1] From the Greek word ἐτοιμασία, readiness (*Trans.*).

Over it hovers the dove. These are certainly only detached attributes, but the closed form of the pictures and the splendour of the execution enable them to convey an idea of the unity of God and the glory of heaven. The *etimasia* often occupies a place of honour in primitive and Byzantine churches, but it was hardly taken over at all by western art.

The struggle against Arianism in the fourth century brought the Church into serious difficulties. The divinity of Christ was at stake and with it the mystery of the Trinity. Artists did not attempt to assist orthodoxy by depicting the three persons of the Trinity on the same level. The similarity to pictures of the ancient gods and the suspicion of polytheism would have been too great. This is confirmed by the very rare exceptions to the rule; for example, the creation of Eve by the divine persons depicted on a sarcophagus in the Lateran. A substitute for direct depiction was found in the symbol of the three men who visited Abraham and were entertained by him. In Santa Maria Maggiore this occupies the important position in the nave; at the front, on the Gospel side, near the altar. The supernatural nature of the men induces great reverence in the patriarch. The middle one has an almond-shaped gloriole which shines over but does not cover the other two. It is as if the artist were already familiar with the words of St Augustine: "Abraham saw three and worshipped one. Was the guest not one in three when he came to Abraham?" In the golden mosaic at Monreale near Palermo (twelfth century) the men have become angels and so remain up to the famous ikon of Rublev.

Christ's words, "Whosoever sees me sees also the Father", provoked some profound pictures which suggest the unity of the divine persons and are of more assistance to meditation than many others.

The Almighty of these centuries is always at the same time the Ancient of Days. The enthroned Christ of the spiritualized art of Reichenau and also the creative Christ of cathedral statuary always suggest the Father as well.

In the sixth or seventh century the Copts began to depict the three divine persons separately. The eastern churches rejected this idea completely, but in the West book-illustrators of the Carolingian and later ages took up the theme and passed it on to painting and sculpture. Pictures of God the Father on the throne of mercy were particularly popular. Benedict XIV advised against depicting the Holy Ghost as a person in a letter of 1745 to the Bishop of Augsburg.

CHAPTER IX

THE ART OF THE PERIOD OF MIGRATIONS

From the fifth century onwards Italy was involved in the confusion of the migrations. After the incursions of the Visigoths and Vandals the Ostrogoths ruled for half a century, and after them, until 774, the Lombards. The East had another two hundred and fifty years of peace before Islam started thrusting outwards, and for this reason alone was bound to take the cultural lead. The history of art shows how the young peoples of the changing West who dominated Italy and the Roman provinces—Spain, Britain, Gaul and Germany—saw

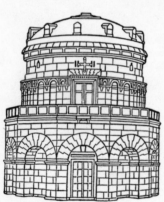

The tomb of Theodoric

themselves not so much as conquerors of the Romans, but as members of the empire, continuers of Roman rule. When they wished to give expression to their power or to the Christian religion which they had adopted, they all looked back to the old Rome, or across to the new one, Byzantium. Thus at first sight the tomb of Theodoric at Ravenna reminds us of the huge round tombs of the Roman emperors, to whom

154

Theodoric felt related and indebted. The immediate stimulus provided was rather by the East. In Syria at that time there were two-storeyed mausolea built on a square base; the inside was cruciform, and the top round and covered by a dome. But out of this familiar form a sort of stylized barrow or cairn was developed for the king of the Germans, for on top of the rows of stone blocks rests not a dome, but a huge monolith. The projections on it bear the names of the apostles, and are thus reminiscent of Constantine's mausoleum with its twelve sarcophagi representing the graves of the apostles. The tomb provides a good foretaste of the synthesis that Christianity was to achieve between the classical and the German worlds.

But the first Christian art fell into a somewhat dichotomous situation among the peoples of the north. A highly developed art encountered a primitive art which had not yet come to terms with visible reality. The Germans had met the multiplicity and threats of nature with the tiny, ordered and invented, rather than experienced, world of ornament, a world that symbolizes search, presentiment and change, not clarity of form. Their rich but undisciplined imagination now encountered on many paths the clear but ossifying forms of the ancient world. From the fourth century onwards hordes of pilgrims went to the Holy Land and brought back with them artistic souvenirs. Monks and missionaries came from the East with books and church furniture. Syrian and Greek merchants settled in Gaul. Foreign names occur in the lists of bishops. The different peoples did not yet think of themselves as nations in our sense of the term and the Church bound them together. The Mohammedan conquests drove a stream of fugitives into the West, among them many educated men and artists. The victorious Germans made the craftsmen and artists of the conquered peoples work for them. So there was an abundance of material for them to see, but it was centuries before any kind of organic unity developed.

THE SOUTH GERMANS

The Vandals, Visigoths, Ostrogoths, Burgundians and Lombards brought with them on their wanderings from the southeast and the Black Sea a style of decoration which they passed on to the Franks, Angles and Saxons: precious inlaid work in bright enamel, jewels and garnets between fine filigree patterns and gold beads. In the Middle Ages church furniture, processional crosses, caskets for relics, book-covers and crowns were able to draw much sustenance from this art. Late classical and early Christian models were copied—usually, but not always, without much understanding—and more frequently transformed (see illustration 34). In the building of churches people were mainly dependent on tradition and the experience of architects and stone-masons. That is why the influence of Rome and the East is strongest in this field.

The Ostrogoths lost their dominance in Italy before their own contribution to Christian art could assert itself against the extremely strong influence of Byzantium. Their historian Jordanes considered the Romanization of his people a goal worth striving for.

The Visigoths, who were dominant in Spain from 415 to 711, adopted the post-Justinian church architecture of Byzantium, Syria and the interior of Asia Minor. San Fructuoso de Montelios was still close to the art of Justinian's capital. Arcades over pillars divided the domed central space from the three surrounding domed areas. The church of San Juan de Baños, with its pastophoria and the horse-shoe arches of its doors, arcades and vaults, points to the Christian East; so does Santa Combe de Bande, with its cruciform shape and massive tower over the intersection. The choir was arranged in the same way in the churches of Vaison in France, Romainmôtier in Switzerland and Canterbury in England. Some Visigothic mosaics have been preserved; they follow East Roman models and show animals and fabulous creatures

from Sassanid tapestries.
The Lombards were
masters of Italy from 568
onwards. In the seventh
century they were con-
verted from Arianism to
Catholicism. They did not
develop such a typically
Germanic art as was once
thought. Little has been
preserved from their Arian
period. Later they fell under the
Byzantine influence of the exarchate
of Ravenna. Syro-Coptic art helped
to produce a Germano-Byzantine
mixed style, an indissoluble union of
late classical and barbaric primitive
art. In the eighth century they
particularly developed ornamental
architectural sculpture. The sym-
bolic animals of the East appeared on sarcophagi and choir
rails. Peacocks and doves, griffins, stags, fishes, rosettes,
palmettes and trees of life were taken over from Sassanid
and Byzantine tapestries. Coptic intertwining bands framed
strictly two-dimensional pictures. Abstract decorative art was
frequently linked with figures modelled on eastern patterns.
The altar that Count Ratschis (744–49) gave to the church
at Cividale is a Byzantine work translated into the barbaric
style (see illustrations 37 and 38). Abstract linear art alternates
with naïve attempts at truth to nature. At this late stage
Lombard art can hardly be distinguished from that of the rest
of Italy. All in all, like the Frankish art which it influenced,
it is an informative transitional stage between Christian late
antiquity and the Germano-Christian Middle Ages.

San Juan
de Baños

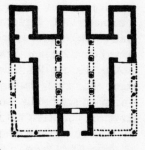

THE FRANKS

There were Christian communities in the Rhineland before 300. Trier was the seat of a bishopric in the third century; Mainz and Cologne received bishops in the fourth century. Underneath the minster at Bonn the graves and first shrines of SS Cassius and Laurentius were discovered in 1928; they date from pre-Constantinian times. Many churches and shrines were built after 313. The double church at Trier and St Gereon at Cologne have been mentioned already. At the same time the hall-like memorial church in honour of St Severin was built in a cemetery at Cologne; it was later enlarged with side-aisles. Hall-churches with round or, more often, angled apses also served the communities at Xanten, Bonn and Mainz.

After 400 the Rhineland towns were captured by the Germans and largely destroyed. The Merovingian age (400–751) was made sombre by murder and the wanton violence of the powerful, but that is not its real history. What is more important is that after the over-organized unitary state of the Romans an agricultural tribal federation under the leadership of the aristocracy grew up, and that monasteries began to act as centres of prayer, charity and culture.

In 496 the Franks accepted baptism from Bishop Remigius and allied themselves, not with Theodoric's Arian Ostrogoths, but with southern Gaul and Rome. Through the conquest of Gaul they came into contact with Mediterranean art. Until 550 Aquitania, with its late classical ,Syro-Coptic inspired culture, was the headquarters of Merovingian art; after that date the north-western and eastern regions, Neustria and Austrasia, became more important. In church architecture, ideas from East and West Rome, Syria and Africa were utilized, but they were never transformed into an organically unified style. Some Merovingian churches have been wholly or partly preserved in Burgundy, which was incorporated in the Frankish federation between 532 and 534. St Pierre at Vienne dates from the fifth century; it is a basilica with columns. The exterior walls are tautened with imitation arches, as in the case of San Simpliciano at Milan. Then there is St Pierre at Geneva, St Maurice in the Valais and a church at Lyon. The splendour of Merovingian churches was praised by contemporaries and attracted these young peoples. Many names still betray their wonder and admiration. A church at Toulouse was called Daurade (*deaurata*, the golden), and St Gereon at Cologne was known as "the golden angels" on account of its sixty gold mosaics. The galleried basilica of St Martin at Tours, completed in 472, had towers outside at the east end, and inside there were one hundred and twenty pillars of precious marble, mosaics on the walls of the nave showing the miracles of St Martin, and over the doors Christ walking on the water, the widow of Sareptha and a picture of the church. Gregory of Tours gives a detailed description of it. At Paris, the splendid church of St Geneviève, adorned inside and outside with mosaics, attracted many pilgrims. In 558, in honour of the relics which Childebert, Chlodwig's son, brought back from Spain, the church of the Holy Cross and St Vincent was dedicated; this was the church later known as St Germain-des-Prés. As wife of Chlotar, Radegundis (died 587) founded the church and monastery of the Holy Cross at Poitiers. In 623 Dagobert founded the abbey of St Denis, and had it richly decorated with paintings, mosaics, marble and work in gold and bronze.

Numerous baptisteries have been preserved or can be traced from their foundations; e.g. at Poitiers, Marseilles, Aix, Valence and Nevers. Some are round, others square with an octagon inscribed in them, as at Riez, whose ground-plan resembles that of Ezra in Syria. A well-preserved example is the baptistery at Poitiers, which dates from the end of the seventh century. It is a tall, broad building with a wide portico in the west and three right-angled apses in the other sides. The eastern one is nearly circular inside.

From the seventh century onwards many circular crypts like the one in St Peter's were built, for the veneration of relics.

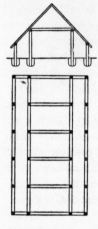

There are examples under St Ebrégésile at Jouarre and under St Laurent at Grenoble. In the Rhineland, churches were often built of wood. They corresponded to the wooden secular buildings praised by Venantius Fortunatus. P. J. Tholen has tried to reconstruct the church at Breberen. The stone churches were simpler than those of Gaul. The long hall-like church, usually with a rectangular choir, took a long time to develop into the basilica. The seventh-century churches of Nivelles and Echternach, and even the eighth-century ones at Reichenau, Hersfeld, Lorsch and Paderborn, all had these rectangular choirs.

Breberen

This kind of choir was the rule among the Anglo-Saxons, and therefore familiar to the missionaries Willibrord and Boniface.

Where Worms cathedral, St Severin at Cologne and St Emmeram at Regensburg now stand, there stood in the seventh century three-aisled basilicas.

Royal courts, bishops' palaces and monasteries were centres of artistic activity. They employed wandering craftsmen. They would buy books, cloth and objects in ivory, gold and enamel from itinerant Greeks and Syrians, and have them copied or given a Germanic twist by native workmen. Roving imagination was brought to a halt by Byzantine clarity, but Syro-Coptic models were highly valued for their power of expression and distance from nature. A good example of provincial continuation of late classical art is the sarcophagus of St Agilbert, with its Majestas Domini and the Last Judgment.

Of more interest to us today are the first attempts of the newly Christianized Germans to render the human figure and that of God incarnate in their own artistic language. The Burgundians had already tried such transferences, as is shown by a belt-buckle depicting Daniel among the lions. A pulpit roof from Romainmôtier shows the affinity of their style to the universal style of the period of migrations.

Daniel

The Rhenish Franks broke away even more decisively from their models and translated the Christian themes into the pre-historic, geometrical style. Examples of this are the tomb at Faha already mentioned and the gravestone of Moselkern.

A small gravestone from Niederdollendorf has recently been ascribed to the seventh century and given a Christian interpretation. In a circle of light interrupted by diagonal rays, Christ stands as God of light and King on a tangle of snakes. This design is based on an old picture of Christ as a general in imperial uniform. The gorgon that averts evil on the breastplate has become a circle, and the cross in the right hand has become a lance, the emblem of the Germanic warrior kings (see illustration 35).

An ivory casket for relics at Essen-Werden from the seventh or eighth century shows in the centre Christ in a short tunic as a King on the cross, surrounded by monsters, symbols of the forces he has overcome. The sides probably showed originally not Christ praying and the archangel, but the soldier with the spear and the sponge-bearer. On the end can be seen an arm of Christ, who on the cross embraced the world. It is the Christ of the *Heliand*[1] and Caedmon's poem: "The prince of humanity . . ., the Lord, the Almighty, bravely and earnestly before the eyes of the crowd he ascended the place of execution, he, the saviour of humanity."

The finest example of Frankish art is an ivory book-cover

[1] A continental Saxon life of Christ in 5,968 lines of alliterative verse probably written during the second quarter of the ninth century (*Trans.*).

from St Martin's at Genoels-Elderen near Tongres; it is now in the Royal Museum at Brussels (see illustration 39). An early Christian theme, known to us from examples at Ravenna, Christ with the cross on his shoulder standing on the monsters, has here been brought to perfection by a German artist. Decorative patterns from contemporary, especially insular, book-painting form a broad, firm, unobtrusive frame which is completely filled by the big figure of Christ between the smaller angels; at the same time it lets the majestic countenance with the blue inlaid eyes stand out boldly against the originally gilded background. The inscription round the picture quotes the 90th Psalm: "Thou shalt tread safely on asp and adder, crush lion and serpent under thy feet." A second, no less impressive, panel shows the Annunciation and underneath it the Visitation in another broken frame of intertwined bands.

CELTS AND NORTH GERMANS

The Celts and Germans made an important contribution, especially to the art of book-illustration. In pre-Christian times the Celts had taken over many forms from archaic Greek, Etruscan and Scythian art: heads of animals and men, tendrils and palmettes. They had developed them into a fantastic array of lines and forms that were partly botanical, partly geometrical. They invaded England and Ireland in several waves, and were pressed back, but their art continued to influence northern ornamental art, as we know from the funeral-ship of Oseberg, which shows a restless tangle of lines and bands, heads of animals and bodies. The free play of imagination finally grew more earnest, the expression of fear for the world, a search without an end. The purpose was to exorcize the impenetrable, the sinister and the demonic by giving it a shape.

In the fourth and fifth centuries Ireland was converted to Christianity by Syrian and Egyptian monks, and for two centuries remained independent of Rome. In the sixth and seventh centuries Ireland brought the faith to the Scots and the Anglo-

Saxons of northern England. Irish and Scottish monks went to the Continent. St Columbanus founded Luxeuil and Bobbio, and his disciple Gallus preached in Switzerland. Disibod, Fridolin, Trudpert and Kilian converted west and south Germany.

It was in Celtic Ireland and England that the old tradition, with an admixture of Syrian and Coptic forms, was most strongly preserved and translated Christian pictures most firmly into its own language. The illuminated capital letters and full-page illustrations interspersed in the Scriptures display a constantly renewed wealth of lines, tendrils, trumpet- and fish-patterns, and snakes and monsters writhing up and down in an endless river. These things are still the expression of stormy, restless forces, but they are controlled by geometrical laws and lit up by bright colours. The human form is completely absorbed into this linear structure. It breaks up into stylized details and as a result looks strange and stiff, like an idol.

St Matthew

Another great achievement of the Celts was the Irish and Scottish tall cross, a form developed at a time when the plastic vigour of antiquity was on the wane and that of the newly converted peoples had not yet awoken. The idea came from the old stone monuments. St Patrick himself turned a menhir into a cross.

The early stone crosses of Fahan Mura and Cardonagh have the Syro-Coptic intertwined patterns to be found in the book of Durrow. In their form as a whole and in their individual scenes from the life of Christ and Mary the Ruthwell and Bewcastle crosses look back to the late classical works of the eastern Mediterranean. The relief style and ancient tendril-work are taken over from Roman monuments. The carvings themselves, for example the risen Christ with Mary Magdalen, are reminiscent of the art of Justinian's age. They display great vigour and assurance.

CHAPTER X

CAROLINGIAN ART

Like Constantine and Theodosius, whose portraits were placed opposite those of pagan rulers in his palace at Ingelheim, Charlemagne wanted to renew the Roman empire. He knew that the superiority of the conquered Romans lay in the realm of the spirit. He was so well aware of the unifying power of religion that he did not shrink from forced conversions. He also knew that the spiritual ideas of power and mercy must be expressed in visible symbols in order to capture people's hearts. So, like all great rulers, he furthered art with imperial decrees and large-scale commissions. He gave the land the peace and confidence indispensable to artistic activity. But a more decisive factor in assuring his success was the young people's hunger for pictures.

There is no such thing as a "Carolingian renaissance", for people did not think that they were rediscovering the distant past, or resurrecting things long dead. They simply entered a hitherto unknown, rich world which at Byzantium was still very much alive and even in the West was by no means completely dead. There was no conscious feeling of opposition between the native and the alien. Carolingian art is an assiduous, sometimes uncomprehending, sometimes magnificent assimilation of Christian late antiquity. A completely successful fusion with Germanic art was not yet achieved, but inspired individual solutions gave a hint of what was to come. Typical of the period is its architecture.

164

THE PALACE CHAPEL

The palace chapel links Aachen with Ravenna, Byzantium
and Antioch. San Vitale is the building most closely related to
it. Yet the architect, Otto of Metz, created something new. The
comfortable rotunda has become a stark, strong octagon, with
an eight-sided Gothic vault instead of a dome. The lower
storey is a vigorous freestone building reminiscent of Roman
aqueducts; its arches continue round on the choir side as well.
The upper storey has lofty arches. They are filled with two
arcades on top of each other, which form, not receding niches,
but straight rows, with costly pillars obtained from Ravenna.
The ambulatory is sixteen-sided. As a result, on the ground
floor, rectangular spaces alternate with triangular ones, as in
the rotunda at Brescia. In the galleries Odo discovered a
solution which is equally good from a technical and an aesthetic
point of view. He supported the lofty central area with climbing
barrel-vaults which at the same time unite it organically with
the surrounding envelope. When the church was consecrated in
805 the two-storeyed sanctuary on the east side had an altar to
Mary on the ground floor and the altar of the Redeemer on the
upper floor. Opposite it there still stands in the west gallery
the imperial throne. The medieval order of precedence can be
seen quite clearly here. The lower region, where the people
stood, is made of strong, unadorned freestone. The middle
floor, for the emperor and his retinue, is nobly adorned with
gilded bronze balustrades, and pillars of porphyry and
polished granite. The hipped dome above contained a shimmering gold mosaic of the Almighty in the midst of the twenty-four
elders. The emperor's position was above the people but beneath the eyes of Christ, to whom he was accountable. The
people stood not only under the emperor but also between him
and Christ, present in the sacrifice, protected and led by both
powers. The two-storeyed west porch had an opening in it,
high up, between the stair-turrets. Here the ruler showed

himself to the people, and from here a connecting passage led to the palace.

There were copies of the palace chapel at the important imperial headquarter towns of Nijmegen, Ottmarsheim and Groningen. It was halved, as it were, in the minster at Essen, and added to the west end of the nave in the Capitol church at Cologne. But its real continuation is to be found in the work of the West Franks in the Carolingian and Ottonian periods.

NEUSTADT AM MAIN

This little Carolingian minster, too, which dates from the last

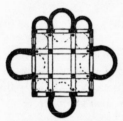

Germigny-des-Prés

decades of the eighth century, looks back, via Ravenna and the coast of the Adriatic, to Asia Minor. This enlarged martyrium is the oldest German example of the *turris in media basilica*, the tower in the middle of the church, as already possessed earlier by St Germigny-des-Prés and St Wandrille (in the diocese of Rouen). The tower, the first cell of the building, still preserves its independence. Walls with big arched openings enclose the intersection, in which the choir is situated.

LORSCH

The small parish churches that landlords built at this time as private churches are of little significance for the development of ecclesiastical architecture. The most important buildings are the monastic churches, which provided room for the general public as well as the monks. An early example is Lorsch on the Bergstrasse, consecrated in 774 and now almost entirely destroyed. It had a rectangular choir and a raised rectangular block with stair turrets on each side of it at the west end.

Tower-groups of this kind were to be seen neither in Asia Minor nor in Italy at that time. It is the first "west front". The gallery had an altar of St Peter and thus became a second choir.

The lovely gateway in the long atrium has been preserved. On its outside walls ancient forms are combined with the Germanic delight in ornamentation. The upper storey was a chapel of St Michael, as the altar niche in the east side shows, and at the same time also a reception room and law-court.

FULDA

The most important large buildings were built in the style of the Constantinian cruciform basilica. Examples are the new St Denis (consecrated in 775), the burial-place of the French kings, and the extensions to the abbey church at Fulda (791–819).

Abbot Ratgar wanted to build these in the Roman style, to correspond with the renewal of the Roman empire and its transformation into a Christian empire. He adopted the huge proportions and even the east–west axis of St Peter's. At the east end there was an apse with the altar of the Redeemer, in the broad western transepts the altar and tomb of St Boniface, who had to have a place of honour like the one that St Reparatus

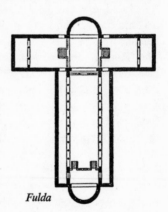

Fulda

had had since 475 in the church at Orléansville in Africa. Both choirs had crypts under them, like the one at St Peter's. Double choirs for different patrons were frequently built at this time, for example at Paderborn and Cologne.

To the north of the basilica, on the rising ground of the

cemetery, a rotunda in honour of St Michael, the guide of souls, was built some time before 822. It served for the remembrance of the dead, on which Boniface had put great value, and also for the veneration of the cross, which was furthered by Rhabanus Maurus. For this reason the chapel was built, like the rotunda of the Holy Sepulchre at Jerusalem, with a two-storeyed ambulatory. There were pictures of all the chief sanctuaries of Christendom (see illustration 42).

CENTULA

Centula is the best example of Carolingian architectural conceptions. The church of Richarius in this monastery near Abbeville was built by Angilbert, Charlemagne's son-in-law, from 790 to 799. It can be reconstructed to some extent from old drawings. Old Roman and eastern ideas were here combined with new German ones to form a rich but not completely organic unity. The ground-plan recalls the Roman cruciform basilica; the elevation obliterates almost all memory of it. The Roman atrium was retained, but the quiet enclosure became a protecting wall to keep out the powers of darkness that attack from the west. The chapels of the archangels stood over the three gates to the atrium, like turrets in the wall of a fortress. The western one was dedicated to St Michael. It was the west front of the church that underwent most change. Instead of a plain gabled wall there rose a huge three-storeyed bulwark with three towers, the first fully developed west front. The entrance consisted of two towers with a tall round-headed opening in between, like the one in the minster at Aachen. Here stood the tomb of the founder, Angilbert, like a barrier, reminding those who entered of the duty of prayer. On the far side of the tomb was a broad, low, crypt-like hall, with a fountain and an altar in the middle again barring the way. The central space offered the familiar picture of the three-aisled, pillared, Roman basilica, but it had acquired a quite different

function. Shortened to six arcades, it was no
longer the holy path to the altar at the
east end, but the altar area itself.
Since the sixth century altars had
multiplied, partly through the
veneration of martyrs and partly
because of every priest's
obligation to celebrate
his own Mass. In the
middle stood the main
altar for the laity, and
about   thirty   more

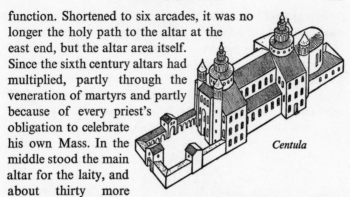

Centula

altars were distributed round the rest of the area. The old name
for this central space, "vestibulum", was both precise and
informative. It linked two churches in the east and west just
as a vestibule links two big rooms. If you looked back from
the main altar, you saw a gallery over the entrance hall which
opened in big arches towards the nave. On its eastern side
stood the altar of the Redeemer. Beside and over this space
there were galleries on three sides which could take further
altars. The middle was free to receive light from the central
tower.

Much has been written about the significance of the west end.
There is no one solution that fits all churches. The west end
served many purposes.

Because the monastic community needed the east end and
much of the nave for their office—at Centula four hundred
priests and monks were appointed to pray for the well-being
of the emperor and the realm—in Frankish territory there was
a tendency at an early period to make the west end a kind of
church and baptistery for the laity. As prescribed by the Bene-
dictine rule, the galleries or the west towers just coming into
fashion were made into chapels of the angels. A central tower
made this section of the building into a real fort, a bulwark
against the powers of hell. The gallery was soon equipped with

a place of honour for the founder, and later for the emperor, who stayed in monasteries when he was travelling. So the west end became a sort of court or imperial church. That is the best explanation of its imposing development with transepts, and galleries grouped round the central tower. Considerable space was required for the emperor's retinue and several altars for the court clergy. The main altar in the imperial church was usually

Corvey

on the east side of the gallery, with the imperial throne behind it at the west end. It was the "capella regia", the royal chapel. The name is derived from one of the chief relics which the court clergy carried round with them, the cloak (*cappa, capella*) of St Martin of Tours. At the east end, facing the imperial church, was the monks' church with its many altars. This too was fairly complex in form. In accordance with oriental models, the intersection of the nave and transepts was emphasized by great arches and topped by a tower; a square choir was inserted between the intersection and the apse as a burial place for St Richarius. As in St Peter's, six silvered and gilded columns, from the architraves of which hung thirteen costly reliquaries, formed a barrier in front of the altar. The square choir completed the cross-symbolism of the church and provided more room for the liturgy. The tower-complex was now the crown, not the end of the eastern section of the church. This also began the cleavage between exterior and interior. The situation of the high altar in the east apse led to the richer development of the choir, the architecturally pre-eminent site under the intersection remained empty and in the Gothic period tended to wither away. As for the proportions of the building, the broad, peaceful sweep of the basilica was abandoned.

Everything was more compressed, more vigorous, pointing up
to heaven with an urgency that was quite new. The six towers
were an important factor in the creation of this impression. The
two clusters of towers were a visible expression of the tense
unity in which spiritual and temporal met before God.

Most of the west ends between the Weser and the Elbe were
built from 850 to 950. The reconstruction of Corvey enables us
to appreciate the austere style of these early castles of God.
Minden cathedral must have been similar.

ST GALLEN

Monasteries were extremely important in the early Middle
Ages. Monks showed the Germans how by hard work the land
can be made cultivable and forced to yield better and better
harvests. They completed and deepened the work of the travelling missionaries. They preserved the spiritual legacy of
antiquity in their scriptoria and handed it on in their schools,
the only ones then in existence. In
the solemn services of the monks
the Germans came to
know the mystery
of the super-
natural
world. In the
monastery, too,
they encountered
the highest earthly
power, for it was here
that the emperor or his

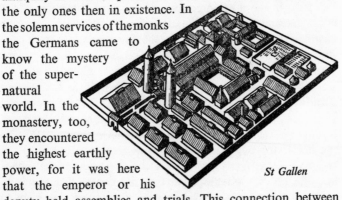

St Gallen

deputy held assemblies and trials. This connection between
earthly and heavenly things is reflected in the layout of the
Frankish monastery as recorded about 820 on a parchment in
the library at St Gallen, a layout that was often followed in
practice. The ground-plan is reminiscent of Roman army camps

in Britain. The main entrance is in the west, in the narrow side of a rectangle about 600 feet by 400. In the south-western corner of the site the *vita activa* went on, farming and handicrafts, in continual contact with the outside world. The northwest corner is filled by the big shed for tools. To the south of the main road through the site lie the labourers' quarters and the big sheds for sheep, goats, pigs, mares, oxen and horses. These are followed, along the south side, by the cooper's and turner's workshops, barn, granary, brewery, bakery, mills and carpentry shop. The south-east corner is a poultry-yard. In the middle of the site lie the main buildings, the church and monastery. A progressive feature of the church is the use of the square under the tower as the measure of proportion for all the surrounding spaces except the nave. No appropriate space has yet been created for the seventeen altars. The west towers, with their angels' chapels, stand like bulwarks in front of the semi-circular atrium. There is a corresponding atrium at the east end.

Adjoining the church on the south side, as always from now onwards, is the inner precinct; cut off from the noise of the craftsmen and the visits of guests, it is accordingly known as the *claustrum* (i.e. cloister). Just as in the Greek house, with its peristyle, the living-rooms were grouped round an inner courtyard with colonnaded walks, so here the open or roofed cloister encloses an ornamental garden after the style of the early Christian paradise. To the west of the cloister were the store-room and kitchen, to the south the refectory, and to the east the bath and dormitory. Near the house of God, but open to the world, lies the hostel for pilgrims, with its own kitchen. This is to the south-west. In the north-west are the guest-house, the school and the abbot's dwelling. Next to the choir of the church, opposite the sacristy, in the best position, is the scriptorium.

The last, eastern section of the site was devoted to the *vita contemplativa*. The novices' quarters and infirmary adjoin a double chapel in the extension of the church. In the south are the cemetery and vegetable garden, in the north the herb garden, the doctor's dwelling and the blood-letting house. A wall encloses the whole site and makes it like a small, well-ordered city of God.

COLOGNE

The plan of the church at St Gallen was also more or less that of the older Carolingian cathedral at Cologne (810–20). During its construction the plan was altered, some walls were removed, and a wider building with a west transept was erected on stronger foundations. This was the "Old Cathedral", which was gradually replaced in the thirteenth and fourteenth centuries by the new Gothic church. It was about 290 feet long. The semi-circular paradise was replaced by an atrium 250 feet long, which narrowed towards the west. The deep well in the middle still produced water in the eighteenth century. The enclosure of the atrium was an open arbour overhung by the houses of the cathedral chapter and the cathedral school. Between the enclosure and the cathedral, on the north side, lay the chapel of St Edmund with its graves, which formed a main entrance to the cathedral. From the

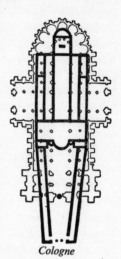

Cologne

upper floor of the living quarters, the dormitory, a staircase led down into the church. The broad transept with its projecting apse and the stair-turrets at each side presented an imposing façade to the atrium. It was supposed to remind people of the broad mosaic-adorned façade of St Peter's. So was the long atrium with its chapter-houses, which were transferred from the south side, where they were in the monastery plan, to the longitudinal axis. The altered plan represents a transition from the monastery church to the cathedral church *more romano*, in the Roman style. It proclaims the renewal of the Roman empire, but also loyalty to St Peter. Inside, a tall staircase must have led up to the west choir and the Lady chapel, for the crypt is here only 2 feet deeper than the church. Its foundations indicate that originally a tunnel crypt was planned, a circular walk along the wall of the apse with a branch to the confessio, like the one still to be seen in Einhart's basilica at Seligenstadt. The model was the crypt of St Peter's. Instead of this a hall-crypt was built, supported by four irregular pillars. At a later period the old cathedral had five aisles. To start with, the two outer aisles were separate areas with floors 3 feet lower than the rest of the building; their purpose is not known for certain. According to the *Annals of Fulda*, this cathedral of St Peter was consecrated on September 27th, 870: "During the night before the consecration the voices of evil spirits are said to have been heard, complaining at having to depart from a spot so long in their possession."

STEINBACH AND SELIGENSTADT

In spite of partial destruction or alteration two churches still give a good impression of the interior of the normal Carolingian church. Both were built by Einhart, Charlemagne's biographer. He wanted to spend the evening of his life in a monastery, and at first planned to build it at Steinbach near Michelstadt. Only the church was completed; it has a short, wide central nave. The upper halves of the walls are carried not on pillars, which were difficult to obtain in the north, but on five rectangular piers; this scheme had probably been adopted already at Lorsch. The upper parts of the walls and the piers together form a firm boundary which is interrupted but not obliterated by the narrow arcades. The austerity of the interior was to be softened by paintings on the walls and piers. The transept consists of three completely separate areas with apses; the idea was to permit the undisturbed celebration of three separate Masses. A tunnel crypt leads to three further altars under the apses and spaces for two tombs under the nave. The church was completed in 827, but Einhart does not seem to have been satisfied with it as a resting-place for the famous relics of two saints mentioned in the canon of the Mass, Peter and Marcellinus. He had a bigger pillared basilica erected as a monastery church at Seligenstadt on the Main. The square intersection was divided from the nave by a big round arch, and from the almost equally broad transepts by walls with openings in them. Underneath the semicircular apse a ring crypt led pilgrims past the tomb with the relics in it. Adjoining this, towards the intersection, were the graves of the founders, Einhart and Imma.

SCULPTURE

According to Ernst Buschor, from 300 to 1300 art was disembodied. It renounced the inexhaustible stimulus of nature, with its lively plastic forms moving in a three-dimensional world, and thereby gained the ability to make the timeless supernatural world credible. For this reason painting and mosaics with their gold backgrounds were the leading arts; in the realm of sculpture, only reliefs retained their importance. Charlemagne brought some ancient statues to Aachen, among them an equestrian statue of Theodoric, but the copy which his workmen produced was only 10 inches high. Relief work flourished again. The façades of altars were often adorned with stucco reliefs or metal antependia.

THE ART OF THE GOLDSMITH

The goldsmiths of the Carolingian age had old Germanic traditions to follow, and were able to produce work that was quite independent. The literary sources mention an abundance of chalices, portable altars, reliquaries and book-covers. Some of these things have been preserved. The most precious items are the Tassilo chalice at Kremsmünster (775–81), whose timelessly perfect shape i s often used as a model today (see illustration 40), the golden altar front by Master Wolvinius in the church of St Ambrose at Milan (835), King Arnulf's portable altar (*c.* 870), and the cover of the Codex Aureus in St Emmeram's at Regensburg (870). A broad band of big jewels forms a magnificent framework for eight delicate reliefs and for the enthroned Christ in the middle (see illustration 47). The way his figure, shaped by the curving paths of light formed by the folds in his robe, comes out to meet the viewer with compulsive energy and threatening majesty, is in its own way unparalleled.

PAINTING

A decree of Charlemagne's dealing with the care of churches presupposes that the bigger churches usually possessed paintings. The tituli, the short lists of contents written in verse, tell us what was foreseen, if not always carried out. The programmes were very extensive. Many allegories which later adorned cathedrals now began to appear on the walls of churches; for example, grammar, rhetoric, dialectic, music and geometry in the guise of the wise men of antiquity. In addition, there were motifs such as springs of life and the constellations. In the nave there were often scenes from the childhood of Jesus opposite pictures of the passion. In accordance with tradition the Old and New Testaments were also represented.

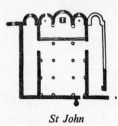

St John

The small, well-preserved church of St John in the Münstertal (Graubünden) gives us an idea of what has been lost in other, bigger churches. It was originally a hall-church with three apses, a plan that can be traced back, via the Adriatic coast, to the Near East. Over the apses the Ascension of Christ is painted, in the

Syrian style of the Rabulas codex. In the middle apse Christ is enthroned between angels, in the southern one between saints and symbols of the evangelists. In the northern one he hands over the keys to Peter, a scene that appears often in Roman mosaics. Underneath these pictures the lives of John the Baptist, St Stephen and the princes of the apostles are depicted, with, among other things, the apocryphal miracles of St Peter which, according to Grimaldi's drawings, also appeared in old St Peter's. Along the top of the side-walls of the church there was a David-cycle in twenty pictures; underneath, in four rows, were sixty-two scenes from the New Testament. Grey, reddish-brown and blue tones predominated. The bodies are heavy, the gestures forcible; for example, those of the dumb man, who bows low before the Lord to be healed. The background consists of traditional designs which are often unwittingly employed just to divide up the surface; they heighten the primitive force of the compositions. On the west wall is the oldest large-scale picture of the Last Judgment. In a circle of light and surrounded by a bigger circle of angels, the judge of the world sends the saved up to heaven with his right hand, and with his left dispatches the damned to hell. Over him there probably rose, in place of the Gothic window, the cross, the emblem of the Son of Man. To the right of the window four angels hold out to Christ, who stands on the left in an almond-shaped gloriole borne by angels, a big scroll containing a record of the deeds of men. Landscape, objects and gestures contain much that is Germanic, and also much that is Lombard, so that experts suspect that the painter came from northern Italy. He gives a forceful summary of early Christian art in all its variety and hints at what is to come.

BOOKS

The illustrations in the sacred books which have come down to us from the early Christian centuries are a good substitute for the lost frescoes and mosaics. They often provided the stimulus for wall-paintings far from their place of origin. The early Church had a well-established book industry at its disposal. There were books before the birth of Christ, both in the form of rolls, normally made of papyrus, and of bound volumes or codices, which were usually made of vellum. In the fourth century the codex, which was much easier to handle, began to displace the roll. As a result, only one Christian roll has been preserved, the Josue roll in the Vatican library. Even this is only a tenth-century copy of an early Christian roll. It is a continuous story in pictures, like the spiral band of pictures on Trajan's column, with an undistinguished text added. The single leaves of the codex demanded separate rather than continuous pictures. To start with, single scenes were simply extracted from the series without alteration, but later on clearly defined compositions in a definite frame were preferred. The oldest Christian codex, the Itala fragments from Quedlinburg, now in Berlin, always has two rectangular pictures from the Book of Kings linked by one frame. At this period the main liturgical prayer-book was the Psalter; for reading aloud, single books of Scripture were used, not collections of the Sunday gospels. About a dozen purple[1] manuscripts with gold or silver capitals have been preserved from the sixth century. Some of them are illustrated. The most sumptuous was the Cotton Bible, written in Alexandria about 500 and almost entirely destroyed by fire in 1731; the Pentateuch was illustrated with two hundred and fifty pictures. The mosaics in St Mark's at Venice are partly based on it. The Viennese Genesis had two hundred pictures; forty-eight of them are preserved on twenty-four sheets. They show a mixture of styles: delicate, life-like scenes in the Hellenistic tradition alternate with abstract abbreviations—for a city, for example—that we meet again in Ottonian art. The charming figure of Rebecca shines in transparent colours against the purple background. Two scenes—her walk from the

[1] For important books the vellum was often stained purple (Trans.).

town to the well, at which the water-nymph rests, and her drawing of water for Abraham's camels—are united in one formally satisfying picture. The Codex of Rossano in southern Italy is very different. It is one of the finest achievements of Syrian art, which eliminates the merely attractive or pretty in order to express the essentials simply and forcefully. Never before have the Agony in the Garden and Christ's attempt to gain comfort from the apostles been depicted so impressively. The creation grows dark, and the hillside is like the waves of the sea in a storm. Christ stands before Pilate in a golden robe, with a big cruciform halo. The deeper truth is expressed that it is he who is Lord and Judge. The writing evangelist, Mark, is—apart from examples in ancient art—the oldest picture of an author in Christian book-painting.

The third famous purple manuscript in this group is the Codex of Sinope, which has some miniature illustrations to St Matthew's gospel. They resemble those of the Codex of Rossano. The best-known northern work of this period is the Codex Argenteus of the Arian Bishop Ulfila, a purple manuscript with silver capitals.

A Syrian gospel-book in the Laurentian library at Florence dates from the year 586. It comes from a monastery in Mesopotamia and was written by a monk called Rabulas. It has four big pictures; the best-known are those of the crucifixion and the ascension. The aim here is never beauty, but force of expression. This codex is the first one to contain the canon-sheets with the rows of figures indicating the parallel passages in the four gospels.

Spanish book-painting has almost all perished. The Ashburnham Pentateuch in the Bibliothèque Nationale at Paris has been preserved. It is a seventh-century copy of an older Coptic model. Its pictures are put together without much idea of composition, but in detail are very expressive.

Sacred books, especially gospel-books, were reckoned great treasures in these centuries, because they contained the word of God and information about the world to come. They formed the most valuable part of a missionary's luggage. For the converted Germans they became the most important primers of art. In the seventh and eighth centuries, the book-painting of the British Isles, which has been mentioned already, was more independent and richer than that of the Continent, even in figure-painting. Its finest achievements are the gospel-books of Durrow, Kells and Lindisfarne. The style combines native and oriental forms. Much has been borrowed from the goldsmiths of pagan royal courts. The Durrow book contains ancient Egyptian mummy wigs; in the Book of Kells there is a picture of the Madonna that points back to the goddess Isis with Horus. Pre-Carolingian book-painting on the Continent scarcely ever essayed the human figure. It succeeded instead in making the writing itself express—in the initial letters—the demonic and the divine. The beginnings of illuminated initial letters can be found in late classical art. Early Merovingian art, for example the influential school of Luxeuil, put them together out of the bodies of birds. Other oriental forms were soon adopted as well: palmettes, griffons and also geometrical patterns. In the sacramental of Gellone (*c.* 750) the school of Corbie developed rich animal ornamentations, with horses, hares and ibexes. The human form was employed as well.

Frankish book-painting did not blossom until the Carolingian age. The Merovingian script, which was difficult to read, was succeeded by the pleasant Caroline minuscule. In the scriptoria set up by Charlemagne, Celtic, Anglo-Saxon and southern books of every age and land were copied, combined and developed. This is the explanation of their lack of unity.

The Ada group is the earliest and most important. It derives its name from a sister of the emperor, who had the archetype made for St Maximin at Trier about 790. To this group belong the Godescalc Psalter and the gold gospel-book at Paris. The most ornate pictures in the archetype are those of the evangelists.

St Luke sits on a festively decorated throne under an arch supported by pillars. Round him are the buildings of a city and above him the winged bull. The picture is based on a Byzantine original of carefully judged line and colour. The artist does not understand how to indicate depth on a flat surface, the drawing of the body is distorted and the delicacy of the original is not attained. But these failures are compensated for by the freshness of feeling, the powerful tension between the component parts of the picture and the child-like, credulous earnestness with which inspiration is made visible. The greatness and dignity, and the spiritual energy, of the man who works in the service of God are successfully expressed.

The so-called Palace school produced for the emperor the three gospel-books of Aachen, Brussels and Vienna. The most splendid of them is in the treasury at Vienna. Otto III took it from the grave of Charlemagne about the year 1000. From then onwards it formed part of the coronation insignia of the German kings. Purely Hellenistic models were followed in its pictures of the evangelists. The ancient joy in nature and in lively movement seems to have awoken afresh here. The evangelists sit at their desks in white togas like Roman writers; the background is an impressionistic landscape seen in perspective. Only the big halo reminds us that they receive their inspiration from the supernatural world. Among the West Franks, the schools of Rheims, Metz, Tours and Corbie all have their individual characteristics. In the three codices of the Metz school that have been preserved the evangelists are missing, and for initial letters ancient plants and tendrils are preferred. The school of Tours usually depicts the story of the creation in strips arranged one under the other. In the Lothar gospel-book it takes up the ancient picture of the ruler again, with an illustration of the emperor on his throne. In the Vivian Bible (Count Vivian was lay abbot of Tours about 850) it possesses a rich cycle of Old Testament pictures. They are copied in the St Paul Bible (now in Rome), which belongs to the school of Corbie. The masterpiece of this school is the Codex Aureus of St Emmeram in Regensburg, now at Munich, which is related to the Ada group. Its most important picture is the adoration of the Lamb by the twenty-four elders.

In subject-matter the Rheims school is closely related to the Palace school; in style it is more restless. In the so-called Utrecht Psalter (now in the university library at Utrecht) it produced, round about 850, a story in pictures in the early Christian style. The pictures are not coloured; they are pure drawings, and very expressive ones. The Germanic art of interweaving lines here essayed the human figure. The drawing follows the sense of each individual verse or word, and binds the many separate pictures into a fantastic swirling, undulating stream of figures. The words of the 101st Psalm take shape before our eyes: "lonely as a single sparrow on the house-top. . . . Like a tapering shadow my days dwindle. . . . Ashes are all my food, I drink nothing but what comes to me mingled with my tears . . . the Lord who looks down from his sanctuary on high, viewing earth from heaven, who has listened to the groans of prisoners . . . the Lord has built Sion anew." Like the text, the drawing heaves up and down. But all unrest is directed towards the Lord, who is enthroned in the midst of the angels and bends down to hear the cries of orphans beside their dead mother and the groans of prisoners. On the right the angels are already busy building the city of God anew. The individual pictures are thus put together again into a gripping panorama of earthly distress and divine help.

In east Franconia Fulda had connections, through Rhabanus Maurus, with the school of Tours, Corvey had connections with Corbie, and Freising with Rheims.

St Gallen alone, in numerous works, developed a completely individual style. It combined the Merovingian fish-and-bird ornamentation with the Irish-Anglo-Saxon woven bands and the ancient acanthus tendril into initials of magnificent splendour. The 51st Psalm begins "Quid gloriaris in malitia" ("Wilt

thou still take pride, infamous tyrant, in thy power to harm?").
This whole first verse can be read in the initial in letters that
grow smaller and smaller (see illustration 43). The illustration
itself gives a silent answer to the torturing question of the
power and success of the godless. The Germanic linear maze of
animals' bodies swallowing each other, the emblem of the
dangerous powers, the symbol of change and decay, is here
forced into a harmonious symmetry, charmed into the clear

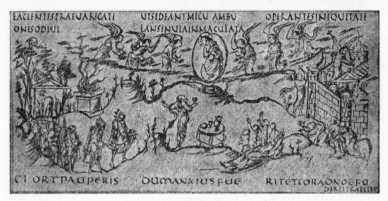

Utrecht Psalter

circular form, and compelled to adorn the shimmering cross,
which forms the axis of the world. Only at the ends of the cross
are pairs of devils, firmly inserted in the context of the creation,
allowed to play like goblins. Gold and purple hint at the divine
power which can banish the unholy. The frame holds the little
cosmos firmly together. The trefoils are simultaneously protection and transition. This initial letter is no less strongly built
than the new fortress-like churches of the period, no less of a
hymn of praise to the conqueror of devils than the *Heliand*.

After 850, in alliance with Rheims, the St Gallen school
developed a magnificent style of drawing. With vigorous, confident strokes allegorical figures were endowed with charming,

life-like movement. The sheet showing Fides (faith) handing the laurel wreath to the victorious warriors proves how swiftly northerners, as students of ancient art, could transform models that appealed to them into new masterpieces (see illustration 46).

Soon afterwards France was weakened by the incapacity of its rulers and internal discord, and laid waste by enemies from abroad, Normans and Magyars. The fresh shoots from the old roots were not allowed to develop freely.

The centuries of early Christian art were past.

NOTE ON SOURCES

Notes and examples had to be omitted from this short survey in order to save space and to make reading easier. Generally accepted conclusions, e.g. about the origin of the basilica, and the Christianization of temples and synagogues, were taken from the *Reallexikon für Antike und Christentum*. Details of researches into the more important individual churches were taken from the appropriate scholars, e.g. Deichmann (Roman churches), Doppelfeld (Cologne), Hörmann (Ephesus), Kempf (Trier), Kirschbaum (St Peter's).

Many details about pictures of Christ in the early Church are to be found in the valuable books of Gerke, Grillmeier, Grabar, Kempf, Kollwitz, Rapp, Schrade and Wessel.

For the interpretation of architecture, the books by Lützeler and Stange were particularly stimulating, and for the whole field of early Christian art the timelessly beautiful book of Wilh. Neuss. The best illustrations to this little book will be found in the two precious volumes published by Max Hirmer in collaboration with D. T. Rice and W. F. Volbach.

But no book can replace a trip to Rome and Ravenna.

THE ILLUSTRATIONS

Photographs nos. 12 and 29 come from Vollbach and Hirmer, *Frühchristliche Kunst*, Munich, 1958; nos. 17, 18, 22 from Gerke, *Christus in der spätantiken Plastik*, Berlin, 1941; nos. 32 and 37 from Robert Schmitt, Darmstadt.

Drawings on pp. 10, 13, 14 after Beyer; p. 37 after Prandy; p. 45 after Schüller-Piroli; p. 50 after Kirschbaum; p. 59 after Guyer; p. 61 after Marec; p. 63 after Beyer; p. 76 after Kempf;

p. 81 after Vincent and Abel; pp. 84 and 127 after Hörmann; p. 86 after Conant and Krencker; pp. 169 and 171 after Pevsner; and p. 173 after Doppelfeld.

SELECT BIBLIOGRAPHY

Dictionaries and Encyclopedias

BRIGGS, M. S.: *Everyman's Concise Encyclopedia of Architecture*, London, Dent and New York, Dutton, 1959.

BUCHBERGER, M., and others: *Lexikon für Theologie und Kirche*, Freiburg im Breisgau, Herder, 1930-9; new ed. 1957-.

CABROL, F., and LECLERCQ, H.: *Dictionnaire d'archéologie chrétienne et de liturgie*, Paris, Letouzey et Ané, 1907-54.

KLAUSER, Th., and others: *Reallexikon für Antike und Christentum*, Stuttgart, Hiersemann, 1950-.

General Surveys

DAVIES, J. G.: *The Origin and Development of Early Christian Church Architecture*, London, S.C.M. Press, 1952.

GOUGH, M.: *The Early Christians*, London, Thames and Hudson, 1961.

LETHABY, W. R. (revised by D. T. Rice): *Medieval Art, 312 to 1350*, London and New York, Nelson, 1949.

MOREY, C. R.: *Early Christian Art*, 2nd ed., Princeton, Princeton Univ. Press, 1953.

RICE, D. T.: *The Beginnings of Christian Art*, London, Hodder and Stoughton, 1957.

STEWART, C.: *Byzantine Legacy*, London, Allen and Unwin, and New York, Macmillan, 1947.

STRZYGOWSKI, J.: *Origins of Christian Church Art*, trans. by O. M. Dalton and H. J. Braunholtz, London and New York, Oxford Univ. Press, 1923.

SWIFT, E. H.: *Roman Sources of Christian Art*, New York, Columbia Univ. Press, 1951.

Monographs

BELLINGER, A. R., BROWN, F. E., PERKINS, A., WELLES, C. B.: *The Excavations at Dura-Europos. Final Report VIII Pt. I*, London, 1956.

BOVINI, G.: *Ravenna Mosaics*, Greenwich, Conn., New York Graphic Society, 1956, and London, Rainbird, 1957; *The Ancient Monuments of Ravenna*, 2nd ed., Milan, Silvana, 1955; *San Vitale Ravenna*, Milan, Silvana, 1956.

CONANT, K. J.: *Carolingian and Romanesque Architecture*, Harmondsworth and Baltimore, Penguin Books, 1959 (Pelican History of Art).

DEMUS, O.: *Byzantine Mosaic Decoration*, London, Kegan Paul, 1948.

GERKE, F.: *Christus in der Spätantiken Plastik*, Berlin, 1940.

GRABAR, A.: *Byzantine Painting*, Geneva, Editions Albert Skira, 1953.

GRILLMEIER, A.: *Der Logos am Kreuz*, Munich, 1956.

GUYER, S.: *Grundlagen mittelälterlicher abendländischer Baukunst*, Einsiedeln, Cologne, Zürich, 1950.

KOLLWITZ, J.: *Das Christusbild des 3ten Jahrhundert*, Munster i. W., 1953.

LAURENT, M.: *L'art chrétien des origines à Justinian*, Brussels, 1956.

MATHEW, G.: *Byzantine Painting*, London, Faber, 1950.

RICE, D. T.: *Byzantine Icons*, London, Faber, 1959.

SWIFT, H. E.: *Hagia Sophia*, New York, 1940.

TOYNBEE, J., and WARD PERKINS, J: *The Shrine of St Peter*, London and New York, Longmans, 1956.

The Twentieth Century
Encyclopedia of Catholicism

The number of each volume indicates its place in the over-all series and not the order of publication.

PART ONE: KNOWLEDGE AND FAITH

PART TWO: THE BASIC TRUTHS

All titles are subject to change.